Personal and Career Development

Personal and Career Development

A Workbook on Self-Leadership

Claudio A. Rivera and Elza Priede

BEP

BUSINESS EXPERT PRESS

Leader in applied, concise business books

Personal and Career Development: A Workbook on Self-Leadership

Copyright © Business Expert Press, LLC, 2021.

Cover design by Charlene Kronstedt

Interior design by Exeter Premedia Services Private Ltd., Chennai, India

First published in 2021 by
Business Expert Press, LLC
222 East 46th Street, New York, NY 10017
www.businessexpertpress.com

ISBN-13: 978-1-63742-028-7 (paperback)
ISBN-13: 978-1-63742-029-4 (e-book)

Business Expert Press Business Career Development Collection

Collection ISSN: 2642-2123 (print)
Collection ISSN: 2642-2131 (electronic)

First edition: 2021

10 9 8 7 6 5 4 3 2 1

Description

This workbook will help readers identify their strengths, interests, and priorities to take ownership of their life and career decisions.

The authors provide a framework to reflect on several questions that are becoming increasingly important among the 21st-century leaders—how to create an authentic leadership style, define one's values, and align vision–values career. Readers are given an extensive number of tools for defining their purpose, creating a plan, and are being encouraged to take it into action.

Coaches, mentors–trainers who help others achieve their aspirations will benefit from the contents of this book. It is also very valuable for first-time and mid-level managers, recent graduates, and newly established entrepreneurs looking for tools to create a roadmap for their life and career planning.

Keywords

self-leadership; authentic leadership; vision; mission; competencies; skills; career development; life balance; emotional intelligence; coaching

Contents

Summary of the Chapters

A brief description of each chapter follows. It might be helpful to go through it to have a big picture of the book.

Part I: Taking Ownership of Our Personal Development

Chapter 1: Self-Leadership and Purpose

In our understanding, the core of personal leadership is not to know how to be a leader, but to live as a leader. We always say to our students that there is a fundamental difference between learning about leadership and developing leadership skills. There are many ways to think about leadership, and Dr. Rivera has coined his own: "Leadership is the art of achieving outstanding results through others, serving others and becoming the best of you." The authors kept in mind this definition during the writing up of the whole workbook. In our understanding, there are three main pillars in self-leadership—three main drivers—that are the cornerstones of the underlying philosophy of this workbook: (1) self-awareness, (2) vision and scale of values, and (3) virtues and life balance.

This chapter elaborates further on the practical implications of your own understanding of self-leadership for your career choices and their management work.

Chapter 2: Self-Awareness: Understanding the Inner Self

The first step is the same as the Oracle pointed to Socrates: know yourself. Before any development process, we should find our natural aptitudes and values, and reinforce them. We must become the authors of our own life, our career, and our actions. Being owners of our own career plans means taking full responsibility for them. This could only start with an objective review of our current status. Self-awareness is the competence, which guarantees an open-minded and honest evaluation of our context, competencies, weaknesses, in-depth motivations, and other factors influencing our decisions.

The chapter elaborates on the different factors influencing our personality: temperament, personal values, and cultural background. Special attention is paid to the distinction between personality and character, and the practical consequences of the differences in training and personal development.

Chapter 3: Core Personal Values

The capacity of self-development is determined by three main factors: the development potential, the need for development, and the attitude toward development. The latter is the most relevant and is commonly expressed with the word *motivation*. Provided we have the opportunity, our development growth will be tied to our willingness to grow. Therefore, the key question is whether we want to grow, whether we are aware of the need to grow, and how far we want to satisfy this need.

This chapter elaborates in detail on the definition of *core values* and the characteristic set of values in long-term successful people. Further, it explains the different levels of values' awareness and the connection between the level of values awareness, level of personal awareness, and level of personal development.

Chapter 4: Building a Personal Vision and Strategy

We can certainly create the conditions for an acceptable level of success and happiness, but nobody can control all the factors involved. *Success happens, the same as happiness* (Frankl 2017). Based on Viktor Frankl's logotherapy school, this chapter will help you to understand the relevance and process of setting a broad *though* clear long-term vision for life and career.

The chapter will outline the most common challenges people face in this regard. The authors will emphasize the drawback of the so-called *dogma of maximizing the choices*. We are used to thinking that the more possibilities we have, the freer we are. However, experience defies this assumption. When the number of options is too large, we could become paralyzed and unable to make decisions.

Part II: Taking Ownership of Our Career Development

Chapter 5: Managing the Career by Personal Vision

How can we manage our careers through our personal vision? In Chapter 4, we speak about the personal mission to energize personal vision. In the current chapter, we will present a practical exercise in order to adjust our career to our vision. In other words, in the previous chapter, we discussed the *why* of our long-term plans, now we will deal with *what*.

This chapter will follow the kaleidoscope framework of Harvard professors Stevenson, H.H., and Nash, L.L. (2005). *Just enough: Tools for creating success in your work and life* book. The kaleidoscope helps users to see the whole picture of their current lives and understand what is missing to accomplish the vision that they have set for themselves. The framework uses a well-grounded definition of success, which is structured around four areas of life's chambers: happiness, achievement, significance, and legacy.

Chapter 6: Assessment of Context and Competencies

For anyone who wants to improve his or her personal and career development, the assessment of context and competences is required. Competences are the observable, habitual behaviors that lead to success in a function or task (Rajadhyaksha 2005). Knowing the edge of our capital of competences is important. A high level of awareness of our competences could help us better manage the context where we operate.

The authors will discuss three fundamental issues in this chapter:

- The relevance of understanding our context
- The distinction between skills and competences
- You will be introduced to a tool to synthesize at a glance our career path

Chapter 7: Assessment of Context and Competencies II

This chapter will assist you in understanding the professional anchors of your career and will offer a starting point for planning the way ahead. The core of the chapter is to understand the role of transitions and to complete a SWOT analysis of the current status of your career.

Chapter 8: Competencies Development Plan

This chapter will focus on how to create a *competencies development plan*, which effectively serves the vision created in Chapter 4, and will become a response to the SWOT of Chapter 7. You will have two important exercises that will help you to define your short-term action plan.

Chapter 9: Risk, Recovery, and Resilience

This final chapter of the second part of the book will deal with the most important competence for career development—resilience. The author defines resilience as the capacity to avoid adverse mental and physical outcomes following exposure to extreme stress or hardships.

Career development in the postindustrial era implies uncertainty, changes, and failures. Resilience has taken a fundamental role in executive training, as professionals are facing more frequently *ups-and-downs* and crises.

This chapter will briefly make a review of what literature understands for resilience and some of the best-known effects of crises. The most important part of the chapter will deal with how to build resilience and to make the best possible use of failure.

Part III: Taking Ownership of Our Daily Agenda

Chapter 10: Life Balance and Time Management

This chapter will deal with two concepts or frameworks for managing our lives or careers daily: emotional intelligence and virtuous leadership. The first is a concept popularized by D. Goleman; Alexandre Harvard has developed the latter. Both concepts have common roots though they depart from different premises. In practice, they complement each other, and they can offer a specific framework for everyday self-leadership.

After explaining the theoretical basis of both models, the authors will propose tools for diagnosis and reflection.

Chapter 11: Growing Through Coaching and Sports Spirit

We cannot live and succeed alone. This is the reason why this chapter deals with the relevance of the daily support of others on our ongoing personal and career development. The relevance of coaching and its basic principles will be outlined and explained.

The chapter focuses on coaching exercised on a daily basis by *manager-coach* or *teacher-coach* or *professor-coach*. Managers can lead without consideration of people's development, considering people's development or through people's development. A manager-coach takes the later stance.

Introduction

The origin of this workbook is the year 2008 when the now-called *Second Great Depression* left the whole market economy and its many manifestations into question. Many managers and entrepreneurs faced suddenly uncharted territory in terms of career and business prospects. This triggered in them fundamental questions about life's priorities that otherwise remain secondary during times of tranquility and prosperity. In many respects, it was a *mid-life* crisis for the global business community.

Business schools did not remain quiet in front of this new context. Across the globe, leading institutions started to encourage the development of materials, courses, and other incentives with the objective to answer the concerns of the business leaders. In this context, we developed in our business school two courses on personal development for our MBA students. Both have proven to become popular and useful. Following the content and dynamics of these courses, this workbook focuses on developing the authentic self in the framework of a career as a manager or an entrepreneur.

The main objectives of this workbook are to help the readers to identify their strengths, interests, and priorities in order to take ownership of their life and career decisions. It follows a very practical approach, as our priority is to help the readers to reflect over rather than transmit *wisdom*. There are other books good for the later, and we felt that a complete workbook was the main gap in the bookshelves.

This workbook gives the reader answers to several questions that are becoming increasingly important among the 21st-century leaders—how to create an authentic leadership style, how to define one's values, and how to align vision–values–career. The readers are given an extensive number of tools for defining their purpose, creating a plan, and are being encouraged to take it into action. Dr. Rivera structured the whole roadmap of this workbook from his research and leading practices around the world.

The core of the workbook is the development of a personal plan, namely *Leader's Journal*, very similar to a *business plan* for a venture.

Through various exercises, the readers will be able to identify career opportunities aligned with other personal objectives while addressing conflicting goals that appear often in demanding careers.

In order to succeed, the readers should not simply single out the part of the workbook they like the most and discard the others, but rather use them as a whole and study each of the chapters followed by an entry in the journal's template that will be introduced in the first chapter. The value of this roadmap will be apparent only when it is applied in real life, else it will remain *wishful thinking*.

The main target audience of this workbook is coaches, mentors– trainers who help others achieve their aspirations. To the authors' best understanding, business education publishers offer a limited selection of classroom resources for personal and career development courses. Generally, articles and self-help books are fully focused on a topic; however, this workbook would link and cover all the main themes related to personal and career development *comprehensively* looking at readers' life and work from a helicopter view.

Further, the book is also very valuable for first-time and mid-level managers, recent graduates, and newly established entrepreneurs looking for tools to create a roadmap for their life and career planning. We do suggest that in order to have a better use of this book, that they get support from coaches, mentors, trainers who are familiar with these concepts to guide them through.

PART I

Ownership of Your Life

CHAPTER 1

Self-Leadership and Purpose

Introduction

AMA LLULLA, AMA QILLA, AMA SUWA—one of the authors met this sentence engraved in stone at the entrance of a country house in La Paz, Bolivia. This is an old Quechua saying, which means, *"Don't lie, don't be lazy, and don't steal."* It defined the basic principles to be successful in the ancestral societies of South America. In a sense, this phrase is a good example of the unwritten rules to succeed in any society, market, sector. In military terms, we can call them: rules of engagement. Personal success in career and life depends largely on how wisely we live according to these rules while we stay authentic to ourselves. This is called *practical wisdom*. It is the capacity to apply daily the *universal, accepted, written/unwritten* laws of a specific society at a specific time.

Practical wisdom is the most important skill for succeeding in career and life. The wise person identifies the right principles for acting while he or she does not build rigid structures of behavior. The world out there is full of winds, and we cannot foresee where they will push us to; however, we should have clarity of mind and will to be firm in the middle of turbulence.

During school and college times, teachers and instructors are largely committed to assisting the students in their task of acquiring technical knowledge and practical skills. In the end, graduates become specialists, who know the basics of being a manager, of participating in a decision-making process. However, these capacities hardly guarantee their ability to lead organizations, other people and, what is even more important, to lead themselves and their families. As said before, practical wisdom is the most important skill; unfortunately, there is plenty of evidence that it is not the most frequent among graduates.

This first chapter will explain the relevance of this book and its topics. We will outline the main characteristics of the current context, which impact substantially career choices and which are the differences with the reality of previous generations.

What Is Self-Leadership

Each one of us faces at a moment our *moment of truth* when we evaluate all our most important and long-standing decisions. Nobody can really predict when this milestone comes, as it depends on many subjective and circumstantial factors. The role of personal development courses and books like this one is to somehow artificially trigger this moment.

You have probably seen the advertisement that introduced the Apple Macintosh personal computer *1984 won't be like "1984."* Apple introduced itself as the game-changer, the rebel, the one who comes to reinstate the rules. Our aforementioned *moments of truth* are somehow a reaction to our usual long-term compliance with the rules of the game. We move fast in our careers, and the tendency is to go with the flow. The question is: am I true to myself? And that is exactly the question we are posting in this first part of the book.

Self-leadership starts with the clear articulation of who we are. There are three concepts or pillars that constitute the blocks to define our authentic self: self-awareness, the scale of values, and vision (see figure 1.1). We will work around them during this and the next chapters of Part I.

We finish this subsection of self-leadership with a definition. According to Dr. Rivera, "leadership is the art of achieving outstanding results through others, serving others and becoming the best of you." Drawing from this definition, we could elaborate that self-leadership is the art of achieving outstanding results in ourselves with the following nuances:

1. Leadership is an *art*, and it means that we need to exercise both knowledge and practical capacity.
2. A leader gets *outstanding results*, that is, even more than what people could on average achieve.
3. Leaders work *through others*: lone leaders simply do not exist; also, regarding self-leadership—we need others to develop ourselves.

Self-Awareness	Scale of Values	Vision

Figure 1.1 The three main pillars of self-leadership

Source: The authors

4. The way of leading is *serving* because an egoistic or selfish leader is a caricature, and not a real leader. Servant leadership is a vision of leadership proposed by (Greenleaf 1970), which has been gaining increasing support during the last decades.

5. The aim is *to become the best of you*, because remarkable leaders are so not, for what they have, but for what they become. Everything we do has an impact on our values, emotional intelligence, and temperament.

Particularly Practical Advice and Principles for Making Good Use of This Book

There are a few things you must keep in mind. We suggest at this point to take a notebook for the first time and write these tips in a visible place.

(a) You are in charge of learning! In this book, you are not just a receptor, but also the main crafter of the learning.

(b) You will benefit from sharing their reflections. It could be enough if you keep entries in the notebook and share them with people close to who you trust.

(c) If it is true that poetry makes people happy, money pays for that. Intently we have tried to keep this book as dry and concise as possible. We want you to be reflective beyond emotions when making such important decisions.

(d) There is enough evidence that leadership could be developed, and we endorse it. Otherwise, what is the meaning of leadership training? Your conviction toward your capacity to improve leadership skills is fundamental for feeding the effort that this takes.

(e) Leadership development topics are generally considered soft. There is enough evidence that the personal and corporate leadership level impacts the personal and corporate bottom line.

(f) Leadership is not about fighting weaknesses but fostering strengths. The underlying methodology of this workbook endorses the principles of positive psychology. A great writer would say that "the task of the modern educator is not to cut down jungles but to irrigate deserts" (Lewis 2017).

Reflecting on Success—The Philosopher's Stone—An Exercise

Throughout this workbook, we have inserted exercises that will introduce you to leadership concepts and assist you with developing leadership skills. In all tasks, we encourage you to think deeply, be honest with yourself, and go beyond the first impressions. Now, we get into the first exercise.

Reflecting on success is an exercise to help you get the awareness of your understanding of leadership and success in real life.

While completing this task, people understand the difficulty to be a leader and to be perceived as a successful leader.

First, choose a role model of success; it should be someone you know personally (relative, friend, colleague, etc.). Describe him or her briefly.

_____

_____

_____

_____

_____

Next, answer the following questions:

- By what criteria he or she been deemed successful.

_____

_____

_____

_____

- How has he or she used his or her success, personally and publicly?

_____

_____

_____

_____

- What problem/s, if any, do you perceive with his or her success?

_____

_____

- *What are your takeaways for your own self-development?*

Challenges for Becoming Successful in the 21st Century

Probably, *success* as a question is a new phenomenon, at least as a shared question by a large portion of the population. For centuries, the range of life choices was very limited for most individuals. Technology, globalization, wealth, social progress, and other key drivers have boosted the alternatives for most of us. For our contemporaries, success as an outcome now became less of a fate and more of a consequence of personal decisions. In our understanding, this is the largest shift in the new context—personal choices now matter—we can impact our life and career success.

Following Professor Nuria Chinchilla from IESE (2013), we see other new challenges our generation needs to deal with:

1. *An era of quick changes:* The speed of changes has substantially increased, which makes it more difficult the possibility to settle and the capacity to decide what is relevant in the long run for our own development.

2. *Inflation of information:* The amount of information we receive each day is enormous and leads to the scarcity of time for reflection. It hinders, therefore, leaders' capacity to understand the big picture.

3. *Career success impact on satisfaction with life:* There is no convincing evidence that the current rhythm of our careers and their price in terms of personal sacrifice make sense regarding our level of satis-

faction with life. In our work with hundreds of managers, we have found out that there is no linear correlation between the level of career success and level of general satisfaction with life. "There is a paradox at the heart of our civilization. Individuals want more income. Yet as society has got richer, people have not become happier. Over the past 50 years, we have better homes, more clothes, and longer holidays and, above all, better health. (Siegel) Yet surveys show clearly that happiness has not increased [...]" (Layard).

4. *Too much too early:* We live in a generally wealthy society, at least in Europe, the United States, and several hubs across the globe. It is difficult to keep high expectations for the future, because people generally have easy access to things from very early in life. A French mathematician, physicist, inventor, writer, and Catholic theologian Blaise Pascal has said, "Disgrace finds light in the sole which prosperity fails to perceive" (Nuria and Maruja 2013).

5. *Allergy to suffering:* The newer generations have difficulties to suffer. The culture around us has created a break in our tolerance toward suffering, anguish, stress, and frustration (Nuria and Maruja 2013). Without trials, our endurance is diminished. We should remember that career implies too many hills to climb and setbacks to overcome.

6. *Ambiguous identity:* The demand for *tolerance toward different values* has degraded to *relativism toward any value*. In simple terms, many today do not have clear red lines for their decision making. Comedian Groucho Marx illustrated the meaning of it by saying: "those are my principles, and if you don't like them ... well I have others" (Siegel). People without red lines lack the deep-rooted convictions that would ultimately doable the alignment between career and life. We will tackle the topic of *scale of values* at large in a later chapter.

7. *Individualism:* The 21st-century society is an individualistic society with a characteristic weakening of the societal linkages. This makes particularly challenging any degree of cooperation in companies, families, and society at large. This poses a challenge of its own to any long-term career development plans as they require the building of a network of support.

How to Think of Success Regard(less)
Google—An Exercise

The creation of a success plan requires "thinking," using our main ally (our brain) to reflect on our own trajectory and build the project for the future. The key competence is what is called "critical thinking" that allows us to get holistic "points of view" meanwhile we challenge the apparent assumptions. Critical thinking requires imagination, creativity, wisdom, and thinking outside the box.

The Google generation has got accustomed to easy answers (digital content experts try to maximize the user experience in a way that anyone can find answers in up to three clicks). It is hard for people today to have as a habit "the recourse to thinking" as a first step in finding answers. We do not deny the enormous advantage of finding quickly and precise answers from Google. However, Googlemania can restrain the training of our brain to draw relevant conclusions from complex problems on our own. And, planning your career is as complex as it can be!

Try your thinking capacity now! Answer the following puzzle without using the help of other people or the Internet: Imagine you are on a deserted island with no phone or other Internet-enabled device. You have never been to NYC. Now, if I asked you how many Thai restaurants are in NYC? How would you try to find that out? What considerations might be important to answer this question? (Chopra 2014)

_____

_____

_____

_____

_____

_____

_____

_____

_____

What are your takeaways for your own self-development?

_____

_____

_____

_____

_____

_____

_____

Resignation Letter—An Exercise

Change managers used to say that if there is a big wall between the ideal plans and their implementation, this big wall is no other than the "lack of sense of urgency." This is the reason why in severely conservative systems, often, the only realistic way for triggering change is "restricting resources." If we are planning, our career is because we want some changes to happen. Either we want a U turn or we want a leap forward or something in between. Experience says that without a crisis of any sort, we will not take our hard decisions.

In absence of external challenges, the only sure way to trigger a positive crisis is a reality check. All the exercises in this workbook are designed exactly for that. But, one of the most powerful is the following: writing your resignation letter. Please, follow these steps:

1. *You will write your resignation letter! Try to do it in an adequate physical space, for example, a cozy corner in your home. Use no more than 20–30 minutes and stick to a one-page long.*
   Questions to consider
   What do you wish you had done differently? What decisions do you wish you had made, conversations you wish you had had, and risks you wish you had taken? If someone else was coming into your role, what should this person do that you have not done? Which dreams do you think you cannot fulfill in your current job?
2. *Put it in the envelope, close the envelope, and discuss it with a close classmate or a friend. Keep the letter until the end of the workbook.*

Circle of Influence or Circle of Concern—An Exercise

In Stephen Covey's book The 7 Habits of Highly Effective People, he describes the importance of understanding the effects of two circles, which contain our lives, the circle of concern and circle of influence (see figure 1.2).

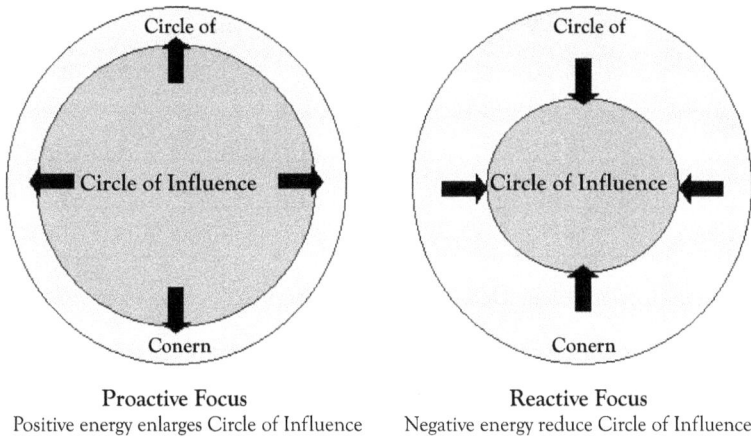

Proactive Focus
Positive energy enlarges Circle of Influence

Reactive Focus
Negative energy reduce Circle of Influence

Figure 1.2 *Circle of influence or circle of concern*

Source: **(Covey 1998)**

Circle of concern—The things we care deeply about in both personal (our health, career, relationships, etc.) and global (global warming, war, hunger, natural disasters, etc.) scale. (Covey 1998).

Circle of influence—The things we have the power to affect (our family life, recycling, riding a bike instead of a car, volunteering, and charity) (Covey 1998).

According to Covey, effective people start with "[...] being proactive and focusing our attention, time and energy on our circle of influence instead of concentrating on our circle of concern" (Covey 1998).

The challenge at stake is to focus our energies, efforts, and power for the greatest impact.

Adapted by Professor Rivera from Steven Covey's very famous model, we offer an exercise in order to understand how focusing on the circle of influence can help you to gain a can win mentality on the possibilities to succeed and become leaders. In other words, how to improve your "self-efficacy" mindset. Self-efficacy is a person's belief that they can be successful when carrying out a task (Cambridge English Dictionary n.d.). *Covey writes, "At the very heart of our Circle of Influence is our ability to make and keep commitments and promises"* (Covey 1998).

(1) *As the first part of this exercise, list all the issues—concerns, worries, projects, tasks—that automatically come to your mind during the last seven days.*

A list of roughly 20–25 will do;

(1) _____

(2) _____

(3) _____

(4) _____

(5) _____

... _____

_____

_____

_____

_____

_____

_____

_____

(2) *Indicate from 1 to 5 the level of difficulty of the corresponding item (concern, worry, project, and task).*

Scale: 1 (almost no effort needed);

2 (requires effort but there is not risk);

3 (doable);

4 (as much doable as risky);

5 (impossible).

(3) *Create the graph with four quadrants. Each quadrant belongs to a specific potential area of the item: family or friends, health, work, study, and so on;*

(4) *Map all the items in the four quadrants;*

(5) *Draw a line connecting the 3s points in the X and Y;*

Example:

Level 1—call my sister, … (family or friends)

Level 2—work on best-self-portrait, … (study)

*Level 3—take my immunity vitamins every morning, walk 10,000 steps/
day, … (health)*

Level 4—visit my grandmother, … (family or friends)

*Level 5—help every colleague whose position was eliminated during pan-
demic, … (work)*

Part of Exercise—Example "Circle of Influence or Circle of Concern"

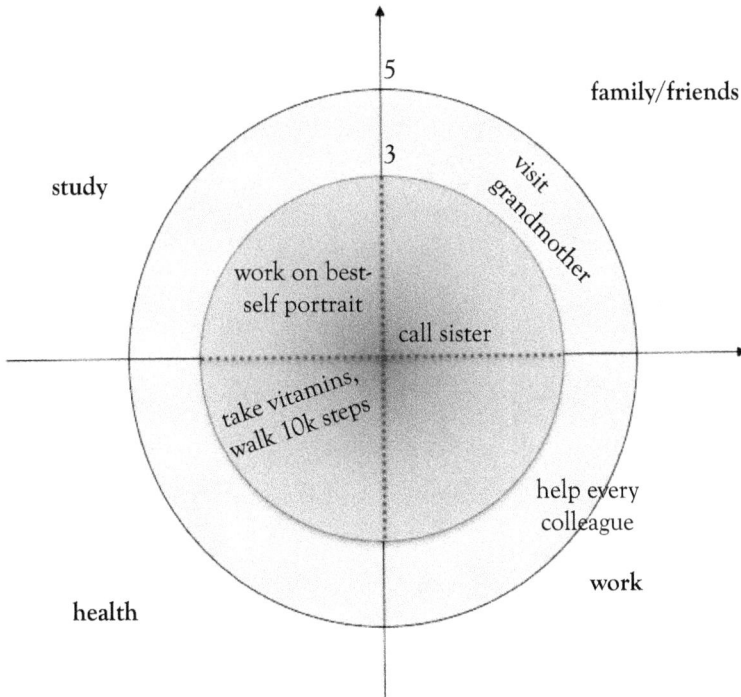

Part of Exercise—Your Personal "Circle of Influence or Circle of Concern"

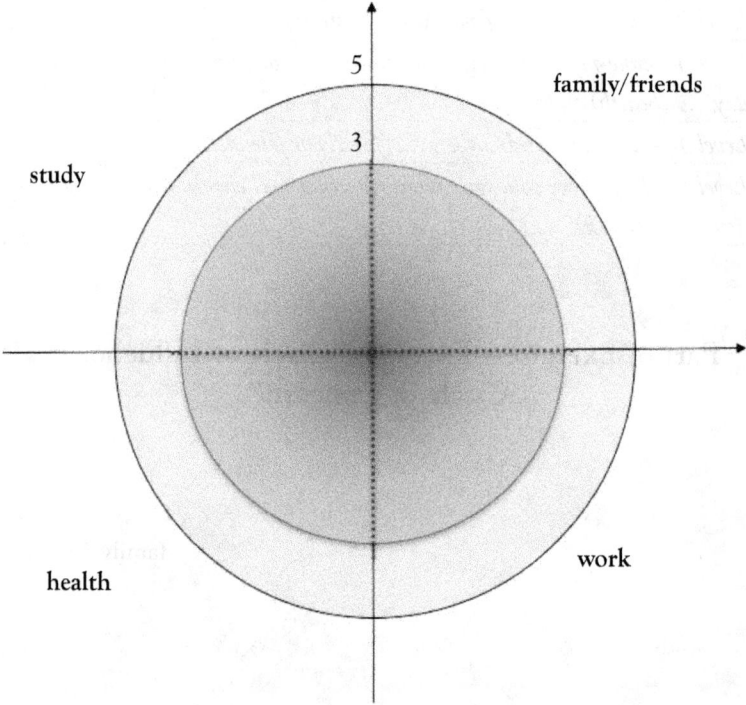

Conclusions

We hope this first chapter has helped you to understand the enterprise ahead, grasp the main challenges for self-development, and kick-off the reflection process. In this first chapter, we have:

(1) Understood the concept of self-leadership in the context of this book.

(2) Outlined practical recommendations on how to approach a process of leadership development

(3) Through exercises, you have been able to understand the level of difficulty to becoming a successful leader, considering the relevance of reflection for leadership development, the importance of creating a sense of urgency to kick-off personal development process, and the impact of self-development processes on self-efficacy.

Before closing the chapter, we want to introduce the *Leader's Journal* that will accompany you during the whole journey.

Personal and Career Journey "Leader's Journal"

This is an exercise that goes across the book and will help you to create a road-map for your career. It has been created by Dr. Rivera and initially intended to be used in the Personal and Career Development course for the MBA students to have a clear development plan.

You are suggested to fill the roadmap following the sequences of the chapters. This helps to think on the topic and then analyze the case, meaning yourself. It is not suggested to fill all sections at once at the end of the book. You will be instructed when and how to fill out each part. This roadmap forces you on writing your own reflections, which is very important to articulate them better. If it becomes difficult to write, the authors encourage you to follow the recommendation of Ernest M. Hemingway: "All you have to do is write one true sentence. Write the truest sentence that you know" (Hemingway n.d.). You can always find one sentence that is true and familiar to you, which will work as a starting point.

Finally, we suggest the readers make a nice printout of the Leader's Journal once it is fully completed. It might prove to be very inspiring to look at it occasionally when the reader needs to take important career decisions. Good luck!

CHAPTER 2

Self-Awareness: Understanding of the Inner Self

First Step: Self-Awareness

Self-leadership starts with self-awareness. Leadership starts with us and requires both self-awareness and the decision to improve our own leadership capital. This is what is called in academic jargon *authentic leadership*. Workshops and training, which are developed based on *authentic leadership*, would always emphasize the development of our *true self*, rather than an ideal substitution.

The key assumption behind is that every person is valuable and unique and, therefore, he or she has something to offer to the world. The development challenge is focused on developing our own personality and becoming the one we are called to be. This is the idea behind these words by H. Thurman:

> There is something in every one of you that waits and listens for the sound of the genuine in yourself. It is the only true guide you will ever have. And if you cannot hear it, you will all of your life spend your days on the ends of strings that somebody else pulls (Thurman 1980).

The first step, then, is the same that the Oracle pointed to Socrates: know thyself. We have to find our aptitudes and reinforce them. It is not so much about finding our weaknesses and fighting them but working on our strengths. This book fosters the readers to become the authors of their life, their career, and their actions. For this reason, self-awareness is tied to self-responsibility—I know myself, I am true to myself, then, and I can become the best self.

Difference Between Authentic Leadership and Nonauthentic Leadership

When people know themselves, the leadership capacity they develop evolves naturally from their existing aptitudes. This is the reason why an authentic leadership style ensues from the authentic personality of everyone. "The first responsibility of a leader is to define reality. The last is to say thank you. In between, the leader is a servant" (Pree 1987).

Understanding our own reality is the first step toward developing leadership. (Gandz 2006) uses the terminology *leader-breeder* and *leader-blocker* to label authentic and nonauthentic leaders. As indicated in the following table 1.1, the latter is a leader who blocked his or her own leadership capacity and the capacity of other people.

Looking at this table, we can easily have a first initial assessment of on which side of the *authentic–nonauthentic* scale we are. As we will see later in the book, when using assessment scales of our observed

Table 1.1 Developing leadership talent

Leader-Breeder	Leader-Blocker
Recruit and select high potentials even if they are hard to handle	Recruit and select easy-to-manage people
Coach for skills development	Do not coach or mentor effectively
Mentor for career development	Lack candor in their feedback
Give totally candid feedback on performance	Fit people to jobs that are inside their comfort zones
Create stretch assignments	Do not establish stretch goals
Reward and reinforce success	Do not reward differentially for success
View failure as a learning opportunity and help their people learn from failure	Blame people for failures
Surrender their high performers for corporate challenges and personal development	Horde the people who get the job done

Source: (Gandz 2006)

behavior (Likert scale in academic jargon), we are never aiming to a precise score.

Particularly Practical Advice for Learning Self-Awareness

While working on their own self-awareness, it is very important for you to keep in mind one of the main assumptions in positive psychology: what is good in us is always more than what is not so good. It might sound a bit abstract. Let us put it in more simple terms: all of us, consciously or not, have been amassing experiences, knowledge, talents, and so on.

In our practice, we generally see that people are inclined to underrate themselves, leading to certain negative attitudes toward self-assessment exercises (even though they externally display an overconfident personality). Somehow, nobody wants to see more bad news about ourselves! We are not asking you to see yourselves only with positive spectacles. We are asking though to keep a healthy level of self-belief.

How we think about ourselves has an impact on the way we contribute to ourselves and other people. Seligman, probably the main researcher on positive psychology, would say that a successful life depends on "using your signature strengths every day to produce authentic happiness and abundant gratification" (Seligman 2017). In order to understand it and practice it, one exercise is offered.

Self-Awareness—An Exercise

Write down how you have contributed over the past week. Look back seven days and write down anything you said or did that you are willing to call a contribution. It does not matter how big or small it is, it still counts (e.g., carefully read Chapter 1 of this workbook, solved a specific issue at your work, helped an old woman cross the street, set your boyfriend straight, smiled at your mother-in-law).

_____

_____

_____

_____

_____

_____

_____

_____

_____

_____

_____

_____

_____

_____

_____

_____

_____

_____

_____

_____

AHA of this exercise: There are many unconscious and positive deeds we do without even realizing them. What happens is that many times, we do not do those things with deliberation, they are rather automatic. Knowing thyself largely starts with knowing our own goodness first.

The Impact of Lack of Self-Awareness—A Usual Case

One of the most common cases we see among the participants of our training is the so-called *alpha male (or female, if you want)*. This term describes someone who is ambitious and is a highly motivated professional, whose priority is to achieve personal goals in the professional field. We are sure that your organization is full of this character!

Many times, *alpha males* come from less privileged backgrounds and have built their careers based on a powerful intellect, hard work, self-motivation, and sacrifice. Generally, these individuals rise rapidly through the ranks, triggering their goal orientation and, often, they end up disregarding the importance of people skills. Without proper feedback, an *alpha male* faces enormous personal crises when they do not manage to achieve their expected and *deserved* goals.

Alpha male cases are exemplary to understand the concept of personality, how self-awareness works, the importance of reflection, the relevance of feedback on self-development, and the impact of culture on personality.

There are three main dimensions that can be used to describe any personality (based on Cloninger et al. "The temperament and character inventory," 1994):

1. Self-direction: capacity to be proactive on career and life development. Someone that is very *high in self-directness* is high in responsibility, accountability, purpose, career goals, efficacy, self-acceptance, self-esteem, consistency. On the contrary, people who are *low in self-directedness* tend to live in denial, blaming others, being reactive, inertial, with inefficacy, with poor self-esteem, and with inconsistency.
2. Cooperativeness: capacity to develop interpersonal relationships: People who are *high in willingness to cooperate* practice tolerance, patience, empathy, helpfulness, forgiveness, principled behavior are recognized as selfless.
   The ones with *low cooperativeness* are known for their intolerance, impatience, criticism, individualism, resentment; they are opportunistic and manipulative.

3. Capacity of transcendence: to see beyond short-term goals.
People with *high self-transcendence* can be characterized as people with healthy doses of humility, self-irony, holistic ideals, spirituality, and without rejection of what is intangible. On the other hand, *low self-transcendence* is characterized by pride, self-sufficiency, individual goals, materialism, measurable.

Alpha males are people (men or women!) who are generally high achievers with a high level of proactiveness, with relative difficulties to create linkages of cooperation with other people and normally with low level of self-transcendence. This *personality profile* limits their capacity to confront short-term serious crises when they arrive, especially if they feel that their desired goals are in serious danger. *Alpha males* seem to live in a different *self-made world*. The problem is that most of their life and career partners do not share the same interests and goals.

Careers in leadership positions nowadays, independently of the sector, stress the necessity of creating an *alpha male* profile. This trend helps in terms of corporate performance but creates very high risks for the long-term *life satisfaction* of the executives who embark on these careers.

Exercise of Self-Awareness: The Best Self-Portrait

This exercise provides you with feedback about who you are when you are at your best. You will request positive feedback from significant people in your lives, which you will then synthesize into a cumulative portrait of your best-self. The exercise can be used as a tool for personal development because it enables you to identify your unique strengths and talents. Your portrait should be approximately 2 to 4 pages in length (double-spaced, 12 pt. font, 1" margins) and should focus on your interpretation of the feedback you receive. However, we strongly recommend that you start as soon as possible.

An example of a good best self-portrait is inserted in Appendix 6. Once completed, please answer the questions in the Leader's Journal Section 1.1.2.

Self-Awareness and the Development of Our Personality

Daniel Goleman, one of the most renowned writers on emotional intelligence, positions self-awareness as the first step toward any substantial change in ourselves that would eventually create a positive impact on others. The reason, as figure 2.1 indicates, is that the level of self-awareness governs our capacity to understand others and to control our own behavior. Goleman looks to self-development through the prism of the influence of our personality on other people, what is a valid point as it can help on making more tangible its importance.

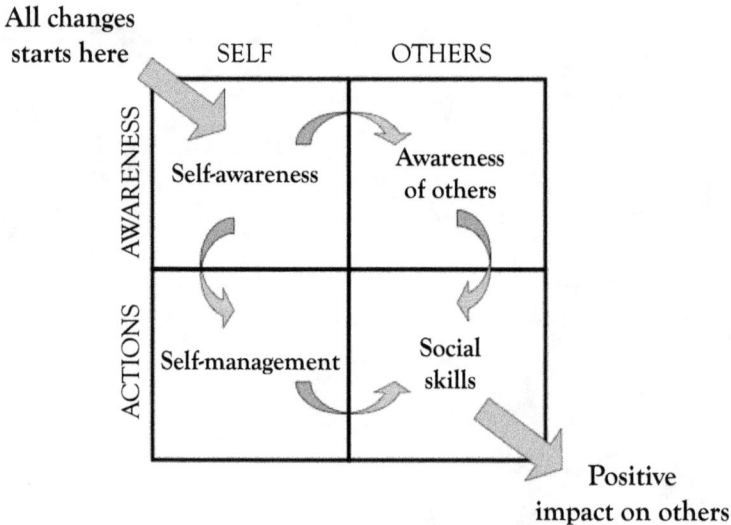

Figure 2.1 *Emotional intelligence as a matrix*

Source: (Goleman 2006)

Prof. Rivera in his doctoral dissertation worked along the same lines as Daniel Goleman: the level of awareness of our personality is a determinant factor on our capacity to lead (leadership capital). As figure 2.2 indicates, our leadership capital depends on our *largely fixed nature* (personality that is inherited and developed during the first years of childhood) plus/minus the *variable nurture* (positive or negative habits that we develop in our adulthood and during the teenage years under the influence of values or role models or crises).

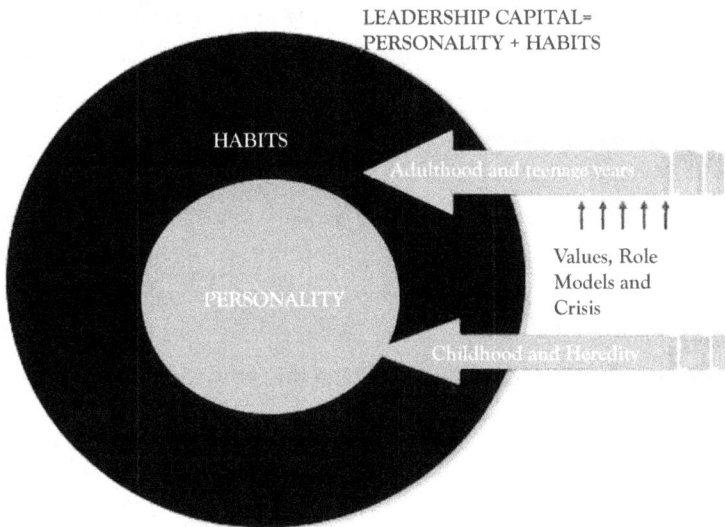

Figure 2.2 Sources of leadership capital

Source: (Rivera 2013)

A wrong analysis (low self-awareness) of our starting point (nature) will diminish our possibilities of developing the leadership capital we need. Kotter, for example, speaks of three sources of leadership that can foster or restrain leadership attitudes: natural origin (heredity and child-hood), education and professional life (career experiences), and company culture (corporate culture) (Kotter 1990).

Though this is not a book on theory of leadership, we want to high-light that there is an important philosophical difference with a large part of the practice on leadership development. Many consultants and instructors set as starting points for the development of leadership skills the needs of the context (situational leadership). Our starting point is the needs of the person we want to develop and the identification of the *authentic leader who he could be* independently of the context.

Using modern terminology, we can say that *personality* is like the *internal navigation system* each one of us has. This navigation system produces from time to time admiration and suffering as we need to work inten-sively on it. Chroningler defines personality as the "individual pattern of behavior that integrates cognitive traits, habits of willpower, emotional characteristics, and automatic tendencies that are noticeable and persist for long periods." In other words, this *navigation system* is composed of different, complex, and ambiguous characteristics that interact between each other, creating the source of every action we take. Human beings are everything but simple.

The main word of the definition is *integrates*. We might share with other people similar ways of thinking (cognitive traits), capacity for action (habits of willpower), emotional reactions (emotional characteristics); however, the *composite* is unique. People with similar upbringings, cultural roots, and professional backgrounds might have similar personalities, but they will not be identical. It is important we understand this; otherwise, we will wrongly apply the different tests we use to identify personality types.

Johari Window—An Exercise

Johari window (see figure 2.3) was created as a tool to help people to improve their understanding of their inner relationships and relationships with others. In other words, it was created to understand our personality! This is a group exercise, meaning, you will need to find 2 to 4 people to work with you.

When doing this exercise, you must choose several adjectives from a given list (next page) by picking the ones you believe portrays their personality. Your peers, friends, and colleagues (between 3 and 5 will do) are asked to pick the same number of adjectives from the same list describing the same person, meaning "you." When all have picked the subjects, all of you must insert them in the Johari window.

The rules for inserting the adjectives are as follows:

Open area—The matching adjectives should be inserted in this quadrant.
Blind area—Adjectives that were only selected by your peers, friends, and colleagues go there
Hidden area—Adjectives that were selected only by you should be in this quadrant, because either you do not know it or your selection does not fit reality (Luft 1969)
Unknown area—The adjectives that were not selected by any parties go here.

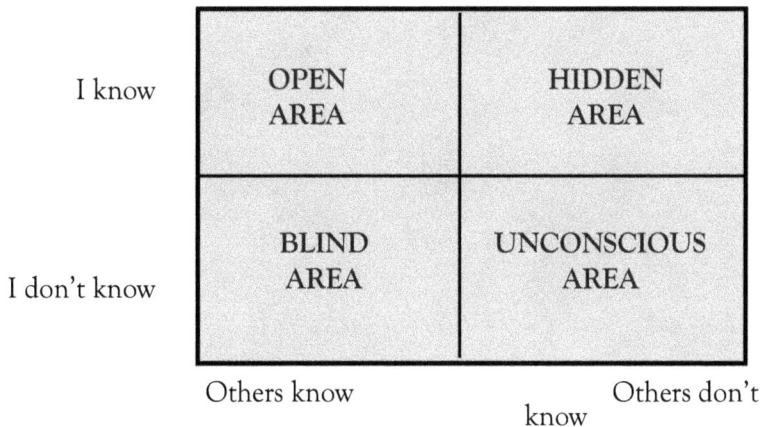

	Others know	Others don't know
I know	OPEN AREA	HIDDEN AREA
I don't know	BLIND AREA	UNCONSCIOUS AREA

Figure 2.3 Johari window

Source: (Luft 1969)

Please, find the Johari adjectives:

Able	*Helpful*	*Reflective*
Accepting	*Idealistic*	*Relaxed*
Adaptable	*Independent*	*Religious*
Bold	*Ingenious*	*Responsive*
Brave	*Intelligent*	*Searching*
Calm	*Introverted*	*Self-assertive*
Caring	*Kind*	*Self-conscious*
Cheerful	*Knowledgeable*	*Sensible*
Clever	*Logical*	*Sentimental*
Complex	*Loving*	*Shy*
Confident	*Mature*	*Silly*
Dependable	*Modest*	*Spontaneous*
Dignified	*Nervous*	*Sympathetic*
Empathetic	*Observant*	*Tense*
Energetic	*Organized*	*Trustworthy*
Extroverted	*Patient*	*Warm*
Friendly	*Powerful*	*Wise*
Giving	*Proud*	*Witty*
Happy	*Quiet*	

Part of Exercise—Your Johari Window

Please do the exercise.

Open Area	Hidden Area
Bilnd Area	**Unconscious Area**

Conclusions

_____

_____

_____

_____

_____

It is important you observe the difference between your perception of yourself and how others perceive you. Your development potential will largely depend on how you deal with this gap (blind area). Alpha males are generally extremely talented people with full open areas but with important elements in the blind area as well. Their long-term success will depend on how ready they are to confront the blind area.

Keirsey Temperament Sorter—An Exercise

As said before, personality is a configuration of observable personality traits, such as habits of communication, patterns of action, sets of characteristic attitudes, values, and talents. It also encompasses personal needs, the kinds of contributions that individuals make in the workplace, and the roles they play in society. Each personality has its own unique qualities and shortcomings, strengths, and challenges. In a variation of the most popular personality test (MBTI), Dr. David Keirsey has created his own test along the lines of four basic temperaments: artisan, guardian, idealist, and rational. We have used this test hundreds of times; therefore, we know how powerful it is.

The four mentioned temperaments are not simply arbitrary collections of characteristics, but spring from an interaction of the two basic dimensions of human behavior: our communication and our actions, our words and our deeds, or, simply, what we say and what we do (Keirsey Temperament Sorter n.d.). *These personality tests are self-evaluation of our perceived behavior, which means that they are not a precise picture of our personality. We always suggest to our participants that they share their findings with people who know them quite well.*

You can find the test in Appendix 2 of this book with the accompanying instructions on how to read it. There is plenty of information on the Internet as well. We suggest that you complete the assessment in one sitting and in a time slot of approximately 20 minutes. When responding to each question, think about how you are most naturally. Do not think about how you wish you were, or how others expect you to be.

For some questions, both choices may seem to fit. In those cases, just ask yourself, "Which one happens more automatically? Which alternative is slightly more comfortable for me?" and pick that option (Keirsey Temperament Sorter n.d.).

AHA. Now, you should turn to the first exercise in your personal and career journey "Leader's Journal" and should start filling in the roadmap with a summary profile of your personality based on the results of the Kersey test— 1.1 Self-awareness and 1.1.1 My personality according to the Keirsey test.

The Importance of Cultural Background

Culture is the collective *mental programming* of a society, which distinguishes one group of people from another. This *mental programming* influences patterns of thinking, which are reflected in the meaning people attach to various aspects of life and which, with the passing of generations, become crystallized in the institutions of a society.

Our culture influences our personality, though it does not determine it. Other factors might have an even bigger impact: family, religious beliefs, education, early life experiences, and so on. Still, our national culture can offer important insights about our behavior and personality.

Hofstede's research on cultural differences is probably one of the most popular descriptors of the differences between the national cultures. It assigns scores on six cultural dimensions: power distance, individualism, masculinity, uncertainty avoidance, long-term orientation, and indulgence. Observing the scores of our culture of origin in comparison with other cultures offers interesting insights on the impact of our cultural background on our preferences of behavior.

Next in figure 2.4 we can see the comparison between two European Union (EU) countries, Latvia, and Germany. According to this graph, German culture fosters more empowerment to the lower ranks (lower power distance), both cultures discourage team-based relationships (high individualism), Latvian culture resists assertive use of power (low masculinity), both cultures restrain risk-taking attitude (high uncertainty

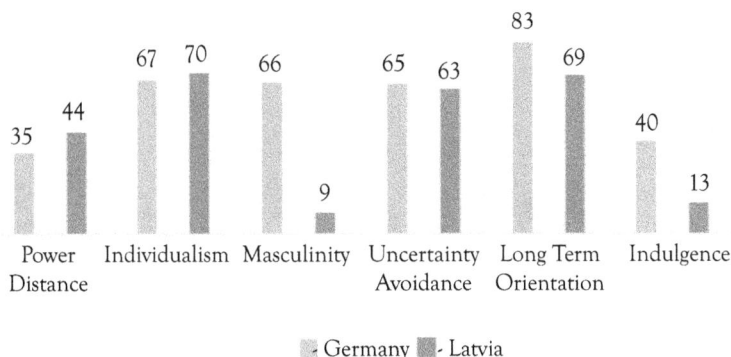

Figure 2.4 **Germany and Latvia country comparison**

Source: (Hofstede-Insights n.d.)

avoidance), both cultures are quite conservative in values (high long-term orientation), both cultures reward hard work (low indulgence).

If we explore for every culture these six dimensions, we can get an useful overview of the deep drivers of any culture relative to other world cultures (Hofstede-Insights, n.d.). For more detailed information regarding each category, please visit their webpage.

AHA. Culture is a very important input in the development of our personality, though, as we said before, it does not explain the whole story. In the next session, we will invite you to assess your own cultural background using the Hofstede Cultural Assessment tool.

Hofstede Cultural Test—An Exercise

You will have the chance now to fill the test. But, before, we recommend reading the definition of each dimension as given by Hofstede. Please complete the Hofstede questionnaire (Appendix 4).

Now, please turn to your personal and career journey "Leader's Journal" and fill in your road map—1.1.3 The impact of my culture (Hofstede test and paper) and the conclusions from this test.

Conclusions—Avoiding the Citizen Kane Dilemma

Citizen Kane is Orson Welles' masterwork (#1 in the American Film Institute's list of Best American Movies), and it remains grand entertainment, sharply acted (starring many of Welles' Mercury Players on the road to thriving film careers), and directed with inspired visual flair.

Chronicling the stormy life of an influential publishing tycoon, this *Best Original Screenplay* Academy Award winner is rooted in themes of power, corruption, vanity—the American Dream lost in the mysterious last word of a dying man: *Rosebud*. A classic to this day, Citizen Kane has only grown in stature since its release, although it was not exactly ignored at the time of its 1941 premiere, garnering nine Oscar nominations, including *Best Picture* (Warner Bros n.d.).

Through this movie, you can see how a person with so many resources was actually not capable of finally succeeding due to the lack of self-awareness. Even though his life changed radically during the early teenage years, the impact of his childhood stayed forever. The movie is very clear that the resources that he had were harmful to attaining his main life's goals. The reason is that he was never fully aware of both his own evident limitations and the most important means to attain his happiness. The cost he paid was loneliness.

During this chapter, we have considered the relevance of self-awareness to understand our development potential and the real roadmap for our lives and careers. Self-awareness is not everything, but it is the main starting point for any serious personal development project. The core concept of the chapter was *authentic leadership*. Understanding ourselves will guarantee that we will not lead other people's lives, but we will work on the maximum development of our natural self.

CHAPTER 3

Core Personal Values

What Do Values Mean?

To understand values, we always invite our students to look at the trolley dilemma (Thomson 1985). The driver of a trolley faces the moral choice of avoiding five people's death by deliberately killing the other two while changing the trolley direction.

Sometimes, with our MBA students, we start our sessions on values using this example. It is an absurd story, however popular among speakers, as it poses a clear dilemma on the most basic ethical principles, and it creates a universal feeling of ethical uneasiness. The first objective of the challenge is to make the students observe that we all have internal principles, even though they are not conscious. The second objective is to make the students observe that we all tend to relativize the relevance of absolute principles (in this case: it is wrong to kill innocent people) if it looks disproportionate or irrational (in this case: killing two looks more logical than allowing five to die).

Now let us come back to defining values. Values are principles through which we look at everything. In every society, family, community, you will find a set of values that is untouchable—very clear principles that are there and come automatically. Values as such are independent of emotions and situations; however, our acting upon our values might be influenced by the context.

Along with this chapter, we are going to study the role of values on personal development. The core objective of the chapter is to understand how to identify our internal system of values. All of us have one. They are certainly shaped over the course of our life and career, but they are so stable that they explain the deepest motivations behind our behavior and, therefore, our personality. If we do not get full awareness of our values system, we might risk the development of a professional plan that conflicts with our deepest, though sometimes silent, convictions.

The Challenge of Utilitarianism

This is a workbook written for the personal development of practitioners. Many of the topics we cover lack sometimes the depth and extension that they certainly deserve. This section is probably the one that would have required more extension the most. Utilitarianism, the philosophical basis of the market economy, is extremely influential in the *forma mentis* (way of thinking) of people engaged in business. Your value system, if you have been involved in business for some years, would likely be largely permeated by utilitarianism.

Since Immanuel Kant and modernism (18th century onward), there have been two different extreme approaches to the concept of value:

- Consequentialism or Utilitarianism
  The value of a behavior or an act relates to its consequences. Things or deeds or thoughts do not have a value in themselves. An action is valuable according to the consequences it has. As a consequence, the value of an action is evaluated using utility as a measure: something is more valuable as more useful it is.
- Categorical
  The opposite of that is the categorical view of values—the value of a behavior or an act relates to its intrinsic aspects. There are reasons beyond the consequences. Therefore, there are actions that will always be right or wrong, independently of the context and consequences.

Consequentialist or utilitarianism is the most predominant ethical approach in business. One of its most popular manifestations is the principle of *maximization of the shareholders' value*, as the main criteria for management's decision making. One of the most popular tools in decision-making process—the cost/benefit analysis—is the most common daily application of utilitarianism. The question is whether there is or not a limit to the consequentialist or utilitarian as an approach of values. Prof. Rivera has written a couple of academic papers on the *consequences of consequentialism* (one of them is in Appendix 5—Publication Transcendental Love Journal).

Are there limits to utilitarianism or, in other words, could we maximize the consequences of our plans, behaviors, attitudes… in any aspect of our life and career? Can we really get a total maximization of everything we do? No, we are not perfect, the world is not perfect. Looking simply at some of its effects, like consumerism, we see how much utilitarianism is mistaken, it creates endless production of useless products. When you walk into a mall, ask yourself what of all that is really needed?

Following P. Drucker, we must realize that "the root of the confusion is the mistaken belief that the motive of a person –the so-called profit motive of the businessman– is an explanation of his behavior or his guide to right action. Whether there is such a thing as the profit motive at all is highly doubtful" (Drucker 1973).

Drucker is talking about the impact of utilitarianism in the concept and perception of success. What does success mean to me? Drucker is suggesting here that a leader is not essentially a person who tries to maximize profit. In other words, a leader is not a man or a woman who measures the value of things according to its consequences or its utility.

The objective of this introduction is to come up with a definition of values and to highlight the relevance of understanding them for our life or career planning. Values answer to *how we see and appreciate reality*. After living in a utilitarian system for some time—as most businesspeople do—it is unavoidable that our way of looking at reality goes through the perspective of utilitarianism. This perspective narrows down substantially our vision of reality and our vision of success.

Is There a Characteristic System of Value Among Successful People?

As we already emphasized, our values work as our internal navigation system. Therefore, they fundamentally influence our growth and development. They invisibly help us to create the future we wish for ourselves to have.

Values are the beliefs people have, especially about what is right and wrong, what is most important in life and what is not, and they constitute the baselines of our decisions. They offer a paradigm of behavior. The paradigm of behavior is reflected in the following things:

- The *stories and myths* that people remember about us, our teams, and our organizations

- The *symbols* we and our teams and organizations use for communication
- The way how we exercise *formal authority*
- The way how we define our agenda, *priorities*, and processes
- The willingness to control or *monitor people* and outcomes
- The rituals and *routines* that are characteristics of your everyday life

The question is whether there are values that are similar between those people who managed to create long-term successful careers. Are there among those *successful people* similarities in the way they prioritize their lives, their routines, their relationships? Professors Nash and Stevenson from Harvard Business School seem to suggest that there is a set of values they had identified among long-term successful Harvard graduates. We think it is worth considering this set of values as an alternative.

Dynamic equanimity—An attitude of giving ourselves a certain distance or space to observe critical moments with more objectivity. "These moments are bolstered by their very ability to step back, view the big picture, plan, build resources, and especially, to renew themselves with rest, companionship, or simple random curiosity to explore the perimeter" (Nash and Stevenson 2005).

Realism—Willingness to concentrate the attention on facts rather than on wishful thinking. "It will get you closer to your dreams than the bravado tales of limitless power, happiness, and love that often accompany reunion profiles" (Nash and Stevenson 2005).

Resilience—Inclination to bounce back from setbacks or defeats in your life.

Integrity—n attitude of continuously checking our short-term decisions *vis-à-vis* our long-term priorities. "An intactness between what you do and the purposes you believe are most important for you to serve" (Nash and Stevenson 2005).

Self-pacing—Readiness to take initiative when challenges appear. "The ability to put one thing down and switch focus not just to the next achievement task, but to another category of the good life that satisfies good emotions" (Nash and Stevenson 2005).

Enjoying the process—Enthusiasm regarding our activities, not only the outcomes we pursue. "Moments of pleasure enhance the ability to do good work and they don't always have to be quite so spectacular" (Nash and Stevenson 2005).

Family-oriented—When their family is one of the core values of a person and their decisions and behaviors are focused around it.

Concerned—Sensitiveness toward the environment and the people engaged in our activities.

Versatile—Different types of accomplishments require different types of *smarts* (Nash and Stevenson 2005).

Humility—Willingness to confront the most brutal reality about ourselves. "[...] not necessarily self-effacing modesty, but rather an ability not to be thrown off by the distortions of a big ego" (Nash and Stevenson 2005).

Sharing—Readiness to share our resources and assets, including those we are currently using.

Defining Your Value Navigation System—An Exercise

In this exercise, you will make an approximation on recognizing the values that guide your behavior. In order to do that, you are requested to define one example (as specific, concrete, and short as possible) for each of these elements:

Stories and Myths That People Remember About Us

(Examples: How did you start the business? How did you get recruited? How do you spend your holidays?)

_____

_____

_____

_____

_____

Symbols That We Use for Communication

(Examples: Motto you use, any image that hangs on the wall of your office, etc.)

_____

_____

_____

_____

_____

Dealings With Formal Authority (How We Exercise It)

(Examples: Levels of kindness you use with the staff, how often people come to see you when they have challenges, etc.)

_____

_____

_____

_____

_____

Agenda and Processes (How We Define Our Priorities)

(Examples: Are you flexible with your schedule? Do you overdo on planning? Do you let other people modify your routine?)

_____

_____

_____

_____

_____

Control (Our Willingness to Control or Monitor People)

(Examples: Frequency and style of reporting you appreciate, level of independence you grant for taking daily decisions)

_____

_____

_____

_____

_____

Rituals and Routines That are Characteristics of Your Everyday Life

(Examples: How do you start the day? Do you have traditions for holidays and weekends?)

_____

_____

_____

_____

_____

AHA. Through this exercise, you could realize that though values are invisible, they become visible through our behavior. Therefore, you can see how real and operative they are. The operating system is invisible, but it is there and acting. Behind each one of these exercises, you can find a certain way of looking at reality, of prioritizing different things in life, in simple terms, you can find your driving values.

Values Scale—An Exercise

The following exercise is a good tool for understanding and mapping your values. Its creator, Richard Barrett, is an author, speaker, and internationally recognized thought leader on the evolution of human values in business and society. He is the founder and chairperson of the Barrett Values Center. "Values together with beliefs, are the causal factors that drive our decision-making. The values that are important to you at any moment in time are a reflection of your current needs and your unmet needs from the past" (Barret Values Center n.d.).

If you are familiar with Maslow's pyramid of needs, you might find Barret's model (see figure 3.1) as a sort of remake of the latter. There is some truth to this. Both models assimilate wants (values) with social or mental or spiritual needs. In our understanding, Barrett's model is more complete as it goes beyond the level of self-actualization.

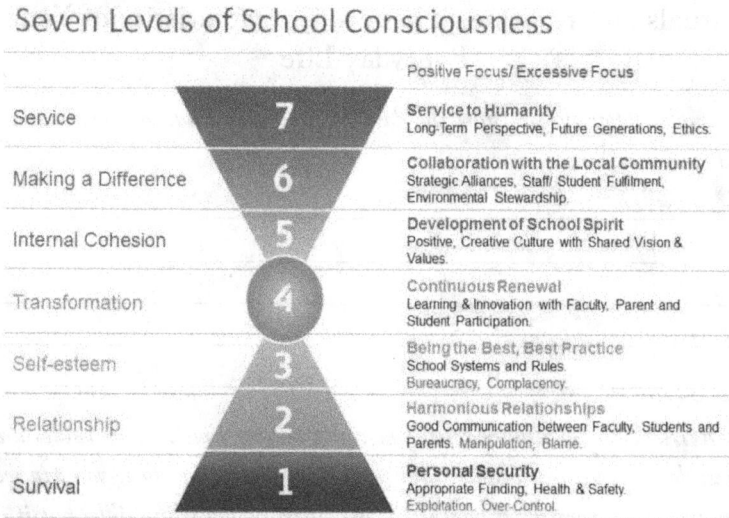

Seven Levels of School Consciousness

Positive Focus/ Excessive Focus

Service	7	**Service to Humanity** Long-Term Perspective, Future Generations, Ethics.
Making a Difference	6	**Collaboration with the Local Community** Strategic Alliances, Staff/ Student Fulfilment, Environmental Stewardship.
Internal Cohesion	5	**Development of School Spirit** Positive, Creative Culture with Shared Vision & Values.
Transformation	4	Continuous Renewal Learning & Innovation with Faculty, Parent and Student Participation.
Self-esteem	3	Being the Best, Best Practice School Systems and Rules. Bureaucracy, Complacency.
Relationship	2	Harmonious Relationships Good Communication between Faculty, Students and Parents. Manipulation, Blame.
Survival	1	**Personal Security** Appropriate Funding, Health & Safety. Exploitation. Over-Control.

Figure 3.1 Seven levels of school consciousness

Source: (Barret Values Center n.d.)

Nevertheless, both models (Maslow and Barrett) are extremely useful when working on human motivation. There is an important caveat though: our willingness to seek satisfaction with our needs, however, depends on our level of awareness of those needs. For example, everyone needs to learn, however, not everyone seeks to learn with the same level of ambition due to different access to resources, previous education, incentives in the context, and so on.

In the following exercise, you will be requested to choose the seven values (from the following list) that mainly define themselves at this moment. One easy way to pick more accurately these values is to choose those that best reflect your motivation for certain crucial decisions during last year.

List of values

1. *Responsibility*
2. *Reliability*
3. *Humor—fun*
4. *Ambition*
5. *Dialogue*
6. *Image*
7. *Life balance (homework)*
8. *Comfortable with ambiguity*
9. *Independence*
10. *Life balance (physical, emotional, mental, spiritual)*
11. *Efficiency*
12. *Integrity*
13. *Want to be appreciated*
14. *Enthusiasm*
15. *Interdependence*
16. *Cautious*
17. *Environmental sensitiveness*
18. *Logic*
19. *Commitment*
20. *Ethics*
21. *Make a difference*
22. *Service to community*
23. *Family*
24. *Open communication*
25. *Compassion*

26. *Financial safety*

27. *Personal development*

28. *Continuous learning*

29. *Reconciliation*

30. *Pride*

31. *Control*

32. *Friendship*

33. *Respect*

34. *Courage*

35. *Future generations*

36. *Self-control*

37. *Creativity*

38. *Harmony*

39. *Vision*

40. *Honesty*

41. *Health*

42. *Wealth*

Based on the values you choose; you are requested to shadow the human motivation level that they are trying to satisfy. For example, if you have picked future generations, you need to shadow level #7. If you have picked financial safety, then you need to shadow level #1. In this way, you should do it for all the seven values you have chosen. Please, if you have chosen more than one value that corresponds to the same level, you do not need to shadow the level again.

AHA:

1. *You can recognize through this exercise which are the levels of needs you are aware of and, therefore, you seek to satisfy. Most of our participants are generally aware of levels #1–4. Again, a utilitarian-based business community has difficult times to elevate the aspirations of its people beyond the bottom line.*

2. *A discussion generally ensues about whether these human needs—in their full scale—are optional or human nature demands the satisfaction of all leads to a fulfilled life. Given that this is a workbook, the discussion remains open, but we suggest giving this question a thought. If we understand human nature better, we will be able to motivate ourselves and others better.*

Sources of Values—An Exercise

In this last exercise, you are requested to think about the sources of your values. Once we are aware of our internal and invisible operating system, we want to also understand how it comes to be.

AHA. With this exercise, you will understand that even though we choose which set of values we are going to use, they do not appear spontaneously in our lives, other people have influenced them. We need to understand this in order to see how to work on them.

Questions to consider

Who has inspired you in your childhood and youth?

_____

_____

_____

_____

_____

What qualities do or did they have?

_____

_____

_____

_____

What do you admire in your current closest person (spouse, child, parents, friends, etc.)?

_____

_____

_____

_____

What do you reject in your current closest person (spouse, child, parents, friends, etc.)?

_____

_____

_____

_____

_____

_____

What boundaries are non-negotiable in private life and business?

_____

_____

_____

_____

_____

What boundaries are negotiable in private life and business?

_____

_____

_____

_____

What makes you laugh?

_____

_____

_____

_____

To get to know you, others would need to know what (symbols, rituals, stories, etc.)?

_____

_____

_____

_____

What upsets you? Look at recent examples.

_____

_____

_____

_____

_____

_____

Using the answers to the preceding questions, write down 15 values that are apparent (you can use Barret's list of value if it helps)

_____

_____

_____

_____

_____

- From the list, choose only 10 values. Write why.

_____

_____

_____

_____

_____

- From the list, choose only five values. Write why.

_____

_____

_____

_____

_____

- From the list, choose only three values. Write why

_____

_____

_____

_____

_____

Now, please turn to the next exercise in your personal and career journey "Leader's Journal" and fill in your roadmap—1.1.4 My value scale.

Conclusions

During this chapter, the most fundamental takeaways are that values exist, but they are not obvious, they are invisible. The predominance of utilitarianism in business challenges our capacity to live authentically according to our values. Generally, we are pushed toward narrow, simple, and materialistic principles like *maximizing shareholder value*. Human nature, however, seems to demand higher aspirations.

We have done exercises to understand which values are underlying our behavior and which are the sources of these values. Generally, after these exercises, our participants end up realizing that human motivation and decision making is and should be more complicated than it initially looks like.

Oscar Wilde would say that there are people who know the price of everything and the value of nothing. There is a difference between *how much* of anything and its *meaning* for us. Our choices should be based on both, especially if we must decide about our career and life goals.

CHAPTER 4

Building a Personal Vision and Strategy

Introduction—Challenging Popular Assumptions

This chapter will hopefully help you to understand how to create the vision of your development process. During the first three chapters, we have focused on understanding ourselves and what personal development means. From now on, the core topics will deal with *how to plan our way forward.*

Firstly, we need to challenge two generally accepted assumptions. The first one is the belief that we can plan our long-term *success goal*—key performance indicators in business jargon. We cannot predict the results of our choices. "Success happens, the same as happiness" (Frankl 2017). This is one of the ideas that Viktor Frankl defends during his acclaimed *Man's Search for Meaning.* One of the most common mistakes is fixation with certain self-imposed and ambitious goals—sky is the limit! The reality is that meaningful goals depend on too many factors that we cannot control. Success is not a logical and linear aim; it is a largely unpredictable byproduct of a chiefly uncertain development process.

The second generally accepted assumption is the dogma of maximizing the choices. It is probably the result of a wrong understanding of what is freedom. Freedom is about choosing, adhering the will to a choice, but not about having the possibility of choosing. This would be the hall of freedom, but it is not real freedom. We used to think that the more possibilities we have, the freer we are. It is a confusion between *being independent in resources* and *using our own personal freedom to decide.* Many people have plenty of resources but avoid constantly decisions for self-imposed reasons. Even more, there are people that notwithstanding the scarcity of resources, they afford risky decisions (see how many entrepreneurs started with underprivileged backgrounds). Maximizing choices does not guarantee our capacity to decide, our capacity for freedom, though in certain circumstances, it can help. This confusion has several consequences:

1. *Regret and anticipated regret*: Due to the very specific, ambitious and, as said before, unrealistic goals we set.
2. *Enormous pressure in reducing opportunity costs*: As we want to be sure we are not missing out in our objective of maximizing the result of our choices.
3. *Escalation of expectations:* Our constant aspiration of maximizing our choices makes very difficult our satisfaction—to be satisfied with whatever achievements we have accomplished.
4. *Self-blame attached to all choices:* The constant dissatisfaction produces a vicious circle—unrealistic goals or regret or self-blame.

At the end of the day, many times we get into a chronical frustration. Against this point of view, there is a much healthier way of understanding success, freedom, and life. V. Frankl would say:

Don't aim at success—the more you aim at it and make it a target, the more you are going to miss it. For success, like happiness, cannot be pursued; it must ensue, and it only does so as the unintended side effect of one's personal dedication to a cause greater than oneself or as the by-product of one's surrender to a person other than oneself. Happiness must happen, and the same holds for success: you have to let it happen by not caring about it...Then you will live to see that in the long run—in the long run, I say!—*success will follow you precisely because you had forgotten to think of it* (Frankl 2017).

The Importance of Finding a Meaning

We are much more than our achievements. Our life has a value that transcends what we can do and what we have. This is obvious and the value or motivation scales of Maslow and Barrett clearly reflect that. The different surveys on happiness prove again and again that human motivation is extremely complex. A very simple scheme (see figure 4.1) might help to understand the big picture:

To Be ◄──────────── To Have ◄──────────── To Do

Figure 4.1 The thinking process

Source: The authors

Whatever we *do*, it helps us to *have* resources, which eventually assist us on *becoming* who we want. Other people use a similar scheme with three questions: *what* (instead of do), *how* (instead of have), *why* (instead of be).

This sort of scheme helps us to put in order our thinking process at the time of planning. Creating a vision on our development process starts with the answer to the question *why* or who do we want to become.

A vision that implies a decision on who we want to be makes it easy to instill the passion toward this vision. This vision should also include the different elements of our life: family, career, friends, community, hobbies, health, and relationships, oneself. Moreover, what matters most is to find a certain balance between them all.

Once we build a vision of ourselves, we will have a sort of benchmark for career–life choices. As we will see later in the workbook, this vision could change and more certainly will change. So, what is the sense of a vision then? It gives us a long-term logic that allows us to keep certain coherence and, therefore, a reasonable level of focus.

Most of the time managers focus their career plans on what they want to *have* in a certain period of time (positions wealth or health or status). Further, most of the time they create plans (do) to achieve those goals (career training, choices, etc.). The problem of focusing on these two questions makes managers career plans very risky. The fundamental reason is that the outcomes of our actions hardly depend only on our actions. Setting up only these goals without transcendental meaning (mission) leaves the manager on a very fragile career path.

Dilemma of Freedom of Choice

Imagine a fish is in a fishbowl. Is the fish actually free?

Given the lack of ability of the fish to live outside the water, it is quite obvious that it is not *independent* from the fishbowl. The issue here is whether pure independence is possible in general and whether absolute freedom exists at all. It is important for managers to understand that all of us are fish in fishbowls (systems, structures, rules, etc.), meaning that we have limitations toward our choices. This thought immediately gives us a reality check that can push us to understand that *freedom of choice* is always on the one hand limited and, on the other, deeper that apparently looks like.

We introduce with this example, the main criteria to design our personal vision: the life stakeholders' net. In the same way that the fish needs to take into account her physiological needs in order to choose *staying in the water*, all of us need to understand the relevance of linking our goals and needs with the goals and needs of all stakeholders of our lives and careers. An individualistic approach to career–life choices does not work because it is unrealistic.

Vision Building—An Exercise

We offer a template for preparing your vision. Many other similar exercises are available on the net, though we created a way that fully matches our previous discussion on the stakeholders' net. Take a 5- to 10-year perspective.

Use these questions as a starting point for your envisioning process. It may be helpful to close your eyes after reading each section to let the answers come to you.

Questions to consider

How I Want to Look Like

Imagine yourself living to your full potential. How do you feel about yourself? What are you doing? How are you living? What other people think about yourself? Which sort of achievement distinguishes you?

_____

_____

_____

_____

_____

_____

_____

Relationships and Friendships

Think of your closest relationships. Who is with you? Who are your dearest friends and colleagues? What do you offer the other people? What do you do with your friends? What do your friends give to you?

_____

_____

_____

_____

_____

_____

_____

_____

_____

_____

_____

Family

Bring your family into your vision. Who are they? What do you do with them? How is your relationship with them? Do you see children in your house? What brings you joy in the family routine?

_____

_____

_____

_____

_____

_____

_____

Work Life

Where are you in life? How is the organization where you are working? What is the quality of your day-to-day working life? How have you demonstrated your values? What have you achieved? What rewards are available to you? What are your main achievements?

_____

_____

_____

_____

_____

_____

_____

_____

_____

Health

How do you feel? Include emotional, physical, mental, and spiritual health in your vision. Which activities can help you to stay at the health level you wish?

_____

_____

_____

_____

_____

_____

_____

_____

_____

_____

Other Activities

Which dreams do you want to fulfill? How will your traveling routine, social life, and hobbies look like? What aspirations would you like to pursue? What do these activities give you?

_____

_____

_____

_____

_____

_____

_____

_____

Your Vision of Yourself

After re-reading at least twice the previous answers, write a short paragraph of the vision you have for yourself. This vision should look like a creative and unifying summary of your previous answers.

_____

_____

_____

_____

_____

_____

_____

_____

_____

_____

_____

The Validity of a Vision: Dilemmas of Success

Once the vision is ready, probably, the question is for how long it will be valid. It is a fair question, given the continuous changes we experience. The value of a vision is not so much about the precision of the goals we have set, as the contribution of the vision to give us a framework for thinking about our career decisions.

During the next chapters, we will work on defining our vision more specifically. The vision you have just written is not more than a summary of what you care mostly—your big *why's*! We will go from this general *why* to the more specific *what* and *how*. It is important you keep in mind that there are four current cultural dilemmas that will challenge your vision constantly:

1. *The meaning of money for you*: This is a very personal question, but we are experiencing a growing interest toward the purpose of our work and a diminishing interest on the financial gains of our work.

2. *The desire toward autonomy*: As the level of general education and a respect for individual freedom in society have been increasing, people's desire for autonomy has also increased. In this sense, your personal vision will be always under tension regarding the necessity to compromise with the stakeholders of your life and career.

3. *A fast-moving market economy*: The lifecycle of companies, products, and professional careers have been substantially shortened partly due to technological advancement. This means that any long-term thinking requires the ability to create different scenarios in response to changes in technology. We must continuously think about how we can be ahead of the curve.

4. *Stress in pragmatism*: We live in a culture where functionality and efficiency are more important than ideals and inspiration. That does not help in the development and implementation of an inspiring vision. We are pushed too much into creating effective plans; however, an inspiring vision needs ideals that can stimulate different and difficult paths of action.

Conclusion—The Power of a Personal Vision

On September 18, 2007, Carnegie Mellon, professor and alumnus Randy Pausch, delivered a one-of-a-kind last lecture that made the world stop and pay attention. It became an Internet sensation viewed by millions, an international media story, and a bestselling book that has been published in more than 35 languages (Carnegie Mellon University n.d.). Randy Pausch clearly points out the most important things in life and how his dreams (aka vision) impacted his professional and life decisions and success. Yes, a vision is a very powerful tool, and Mr. Pausch proved it in his acclaimed lecture.

In this chapter, we have explained the relevance of a vision for personal and career development and how to design it. Friedrich Nietzsche would say: "he who has a *why* to live for can bear almost any how" (Nietzsche 1974). A vision energizes because it articulates clearly our main motivations and gives us a broad perspective in terms of our career goals and ambitions. This broad perspective allows us to have less fragile goals as we do not focus only on very specific achievements that we can hardly completely control.

In a nutshell, a vision gives us a sense of transcendence to our specific plans and helps us focus on our strengths rather than our weaknesses. This is the basis of what we call today positive psychology, which has proven to be very effective in motivating people and companies on overcoming challenges. Finally, a vision makes us focus our attention toward the future rather than in a past that no longer exists.

Aristotle in his Nicomachean Ethics would distinguish between filling and flourishing. His point was that a truly meaningful life is not so much the one where all needs are satisfied, but rather the life where our own personality has been developed to the full. That is what a vision allows to keep in mind and the reason for its power. Seligman goes even further, and he would say that a meaningful life is one where we use "signature strengths and virtues in the service of something much larger than you are" (Seligman 2017). A vision then would not be only about who we want to become, but which impact we want to leave in the society around us. And, this is a matter of the next chapter—making the vision more complete, holistic, specific, and driven toward the common good of the society around us.

PART II

Ownership of Your Career

CHAPTER 5

Managing the Career by Personal Vision

Introduction

Probably, you have seen tapestries (just in case, see Figure 5.1). A tapestry is an object that has two completely different sides. One is the beautiful image it represents and is visible for everyone on the front, but when you turn it around, it shows all the knots and jumbles of threads.

This is a good metaphor for a career. On the one hand, the visible picture of an ambitious career is exciting, and on the other hand, it implies countless sacrifices and tradeoffs only few people are aware of. In the short run, a successful career might look difficult and unattractive, but if the

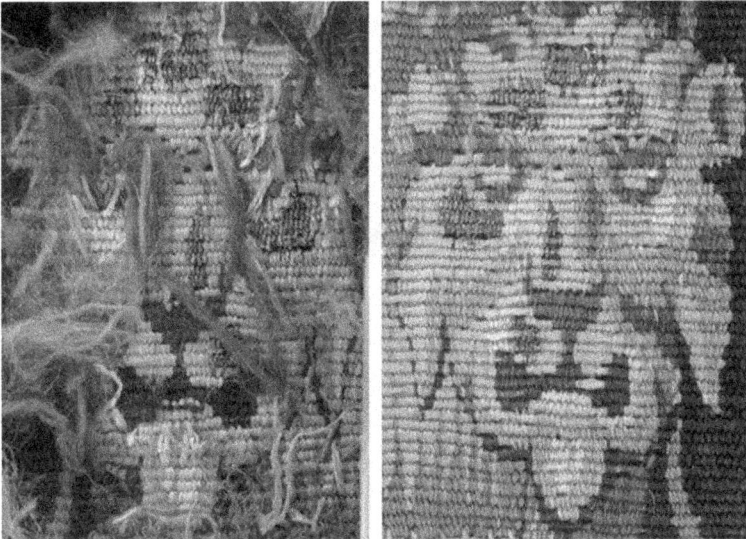

Figure 5.1 Abraham entertaining the angels from the story of Abraham (1600)

Source: (Metropolitan Museum of Art n.d.)

dots are connected and the threats are linked, the career in the long run becomes meaningful and successful.

A career implies many tradeoffs, meaning that there are things we must give up in order to accept opportunities. At the end of the day, all of us are confronted with decisions on what we do and what we give up.

In the previous chapters, we have learned how to create a vision that fits our values and personality—the front side of the tapestry. From this chapter onward, we will work on the back side of the tapestry: the different decisions we need to take regarding career choices, competences, business opportunities, and developmental objectives. We should keep though our vision always in mind, as that is the way to keep consistency in the decision-making process.

Our careers can be represented like a tree where the roots are the *personal and professional anchors*, the truck is our *career plans*, and the branches and leaves are our *skillset*. The land where the tree grows is the *work environment*. In the big picture, these are the four elements of any career development. These four influences the development of our careers, and we will go into detail of each of them during the next chapters.

When we talk about our vision, we are talking about the main personal and professional anchors of our careers. If they are deep and strong, it will serve as the tutor for the tree. The work environment, the career plan, and the skillsets affect the speed and height of growth. However, the stability of the tree is guaranteed by the vision.

Risks of Not Defining a Vision

As aforementioned, the vision gives consistency of the big picture of our careers and stability to the career plan.

If there is not a cautious identification of our vision or if our vision does not become a guiding pattern in our careers, then we might face substantial risks.

Some of the risks are the following:

1. *We might face a hard time understanding other people.*
   The vision represents our deepest motivations and a cautious decision to follow them. If we are not aware of them, we might

have difficulties understanding other people's motivations simply because we generally tend to see other people as we see ourselves. We already discussed the relevance of self-awareness in Chapter 2.

2. *We might develop the wrong skills.*

If we do not have a vision, then it is very difficult to understand and define our career objectives. Skill development takes a lot of investment, and it makes sense to think carefully about whether the skills we are planning to develop serve the right purpose.

3. *We might develop only what the system (aka job market) requires.*

A vision guarantees a proactive approach toward career decisions. The alternative is just to become reactive to whatever the system requires from us. It means that our career is not driven by us, but is driven by the *hidden* hand of the market. Though it is important to observe what companies require to adjust to the system, it is also important to have a feeling of self-determination of our careers. (Please, watch video *RSA Animate: Drive: The surprising truth about what motivates us.*)

4. *We can be trapped in the wrong career.*

Once we access a specific career path, we can become part of the system; however, after a certain time, the possibilities of changing our career path become increasingly more difficult.

The Kaleidoscope Strategy and a Definition of Success

The kaleidoscope is an old-school mechanical device that you hold up to the light and play with. It has four separate chambers, colored chips, and mirrors, which form ever-changing patterns when you are turning the end of the tube (Nash and Stevenson 2005).

Following Harvard professors Nash and Stevenson (2005), we will use the kaleidoscope as an image, a framework, of our own life. The colored chips are our regular activities; meanwhile, the chambers are the different categories of our life. Hence, different combinations of activities will produce different *visible shapes of our life* through four different chambers of our lives: achievement, legacy, happiness, and significance. It is what Nash and Stevenson call the *kaleidoscope strategy*. The definitions they give to the different categories are:

- Happiness: Feelings of pleasure and contentment in and about your life
- Achievement: Accomplishment that compare favorably against similar goals others have strived for
- Significance: A positive impact on people you care about
- Legacy: Establishing your values or accomplishments in ways that help others find future success (Nash and Stevenson 2005)

The kaleidoscope strategy is a framework we have been using extensively to help the participants of our programs to understand how to decide the tradeoffs of our careers and align our activities with our vision and life's bigger picture. Before we proceed to an exercise to understand it, it is important to clarify that the kaleidoscope strategy assumes a very specific understanding of what a *successful life* is.

According to Nash and Stevenson, an *enduring* successful life consists of "a collection of activities viewed affirmatively by you and those you care about, now, throughout your life, and beyond," This definition has important consequences that the authors of this workbook consider valid to mention, as they challenge the general conception people have of success:

1. Success is not the sum of certain goals that have been achieved. Rather, success is the sum of certain activities we regularly run. In other words, what is important is the process, not the outcome.
2. This collection of activities should be *viewed affirmatively*. It means that the perception we have of these activities is as important as the activities themselves.
3. Our perception of success will also depend on the appreciation of our activities by our beloved ones. A person is a social being, we cannot handle our decisions only on our own.
4. The long-term impact of our activities is relevant for perceiving them as successful. That is the reason why the definition highlights "now, throughout your life, and beyond." In a society where immediate satisfaction is so relevant, this perspective is a challenge to the general mindset.

"Whatever you cannot understand you cannot possess" (Von Goethe 1853). The concept of the kaleidoscope and the definition of *enduring success* highlight the relevance of reflection: in order to be successful, understanding the meaning of our activities is as important as the activities themselves. In the next session, we will clarify further the kaleidoscope strategy through an exercise.

Kaleidoscope Strategy—An Exercise

In this exercise, you will be asked to implement the kaleidoscope strategy based on the book Just Enough: Tools for Creating Success in Your Work and Life (Nash and Stevenson 2005). Dr. Rivera has developed an in-class exercise to use the kaleidoscope framework as part of the Personal and Career Development course at Riga Business School. This exercise follows the essential elements of the kaleidoscope, though it has been adapted to the classroom setting in order to allow the implementation of the exercise and the debriefing in the time slot of three hours in total.

Before you start: we assume you have already written the vision, as indicated in Chapter 4. Now you should follow these steps:

1. *List your most regular activities. No less than 15–20 activities. These are the activities you do daily, weekly, monthly, annually, and are not immediately obvious, for example, sleeping, eating and so forth. Napping once a week in the garden is a regular activity, eating Sunday dinner with family is another. Regular activities can be in and out of professional settings. Example: riding a bike, reading, gardening, cooking dinner for family, meeting friends, taking a bath, going to church, doing homework, doing chords, going to the gym, visiting your parents, traveling, visiting an animal shelter or other types of charity work, donating blood, going to hairdressers, helping a colleague, washing your car, buying new clothes, going to the beach, voting in elections, going through training, and so on.*

   _____

   _____

   _____

   _____

   _____

   _____

   _____

   _____

   _____

   _____

   _____

2. *Indicate up to two real beneficiaries of each one of your activities. They should be one or two of the following: self, family, work, or community. Example: riding a bike (self), reading (self), gardening (self), cooking dinner for family (self, family), and donating blood (community).*

_____

_____

_____

_____

_____

_____

_____

_____

_____

_____

_____

_____

_____

_____

_____

_____

_____

3. *Indicate up to two outcomes (chambers) of each one of the activities (happiness, achievement, significance, or legacy). Please, review the definitions of the chambers previous to this task. Example: riding a bike (self, happiness), reading (self, happiness), gardening (self, happiness), cooking dinner for family (self, family, and significance), donating blood (community, legacy).*

_____

_____

_____

_____

_____

_____
_____
_____
_____
_____
_____
_____
_____
_____
_____
_____
_____
_____
_____

4. *Draw the kaleidoscope (see figure 5.2). Put the activities you listed earlier into their correspondent space.*

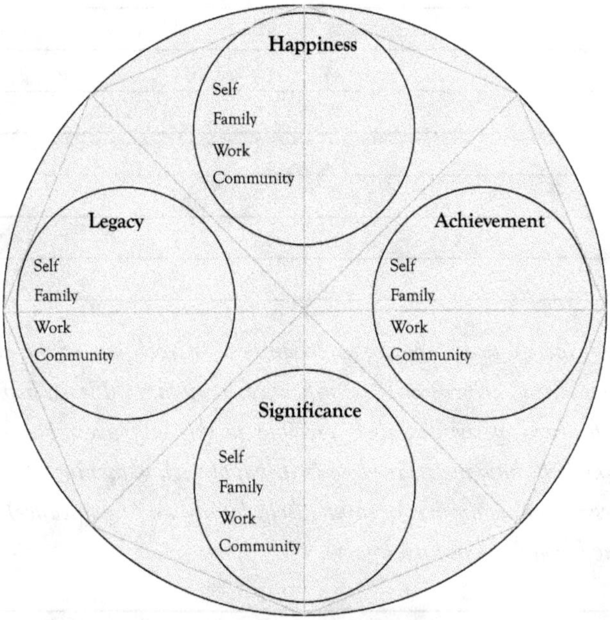

Figure 5.2 Your four successes: A worksheet

Source: (Nash and Stevenson 2005)

5. *Finally, it is time to analyze your personal kaleidoscope.*

Questions to consider

Are some chambers empty? Are others too full? Where are you devoting most of your time? Is that in line with your vision?

_____

_____

_____

_____

_____

_____

_____

_____

Now, please turn to the exercise in your personal and career journey "Leader's Journal" and start filling in your roadmap—1.2. My Kaleidoscope. When you have done the test, please fill out the conclusions from this test.

Debriefing the Kaleidoscope

How can we manage our career by our personal vision? In the last two chapters, we have at length discussed the relevance of defining the vision for our career success. The kaleidoscope strategy is an excellent tool to understand how aligned our current activities are with our desired vision. In a way, the kaleidoscope displays our real vision—we like it or not!

If your kaleidoscope is well balanced and in line with your vision, then congratulations, because it means that you are on the right path. If it is not, then you should consider the possibility of spending your time in a different way, hence changing your activities.

We have limited time; the question is what would be enough for us to be satisfied. We cannot keep all the chambers full; we cannot leave chambers empty either, as success implies a certain level of balance. Seeing success as a question of tradeoffs and equilibrium counters the popular idea that success depends on passion and focus. The latter is based on a wrong conception of the human being, and they lead to the most common problems of success today: stress, burnout, personal disappointment, and indecision. This is the reason why we have always been relatively suspicious of the wisdom of a *start-up* career style.

On the contrary, according to Nash and Stevenson (2005), the characteristics of long-term achievers are in alignment with the previously mentioned definition of *enduring success*:

- Outward and varied success
- Multiple goals
- Positive contribution
- In it for the long term
- Autonomy or empathy balance

These values fit the current trends of aligning the corporate world with the global aspirations of taking care of our planet's sustainability, social justice, and well-being of the poorest. United Nations has defined the so-called Sustainable Development Goals, and they require a commitment of all the main forces of our societies, including business. We need leaders who responsibly lead themselves and their organizations.

Leading with responsibility implies considering the long term, being empathetic toward society's needs, trying to impact the context positively, and not reducing the management work to a very narrow set of goals. Frameworks like the kaleidoscope can certainly help leaders have a reality check of how their current careers fit this aspiration of *responsible leadership.*

Conclusions—a Systematic Way of Framing Our Vision

This chapter has been a bridge between *defining our ideal* (vision) and making our ideal concrete and specific in our goals and activities. We cannot do that only with intuition, and that is the reason why we offer a framework (kaleidoscope strategy). A framework is always limited and somehow on abstract representation of reality. However, a framework, if well-designed, has always the capacity to help us refine our intuition considering the main elements of the reality under analysis. In our case, the kaleidoscope strategy can help us describe the current reality of our life or career in a holistic and research-based way.

Behind the kaleidoscope strategy, there are important assumptions you could agree or disagree upon but where there is strong empirical evidence. The first one is the understanding of success as the result of choosing activities rather than relying on outcomes. This definition is in full alignment with our previous cited definition of Victor Frankl where success is considered as a byproduct. The second assumption is that a successful life implies choosing several activities that keep our life in balance in its different sides. As Nash and Stevenson said: "the core message is that success is not about one thing nor an infinite number of things; it is about 'just enough.'" This perspective is in alignment with defining our vision taking into account a stakeholder perspective and limiting our ambition of maximizing choices.

Before concluding this chapter, using the Gallup World Poll (Cantril ladder), we will ask you to quickly *calculate* your current level of *perceived happiness* or rather of *enduring success*:

Please, imagine a ladder with steps numbered from zero at the bottom to 10 at the top. Suppose we say that the top of the ladder represents the best possible life for you and the bottom of the ladder represents the worst possible life for you.

On which step of the ladder would you say you personally feel you stand at this time, assuming the higher the step, the better you feel about your life, and the lower the step the worse you feel about it? Which step comes closest to the way you feel?

Please, be advised that our audiences are generally composed of better-off people. The reasons—the problems around success today: stress, burnout, personal disappointment, and indecision, lack of balance between life and career goals, and so on.

The answers to those problems are not neither simple nor purely intuitive. And, as Nash and Stevenson say, the "key to this complexity is alignment and calibration." In order to do that, we need a tool, a disciplined framework, and an inspiring vision.

CHAPTER 6

Assessment of Context and Competencies

Introduction

Now that we have clarity regarding our life's main goals in the framework of our vision, we need to start setting up our career's plan. As with any business plan, at the time of developing our business career, we need to have an awareness of the context of the market where we run it. A career in itself can be considered a company that also requires a strengths, weaknesses, opportunities, threats (SWOT) analysis based on the context.

Though it is generally known, we want to remind you that we live in the postindustrial era, where the skills and competencies that are demanded from the market are essentially different from those that were requested in the 19th and 20th centuries. The knowledge society requires ever more the so-called nonroutine skills, given the level of automation and the increasing complexity of the problems private and public sectors deal with.

As you can see in figure 6.1, there is an increasing demand for higher-order skills in the labor market like critical thinking, interpersonal skills,

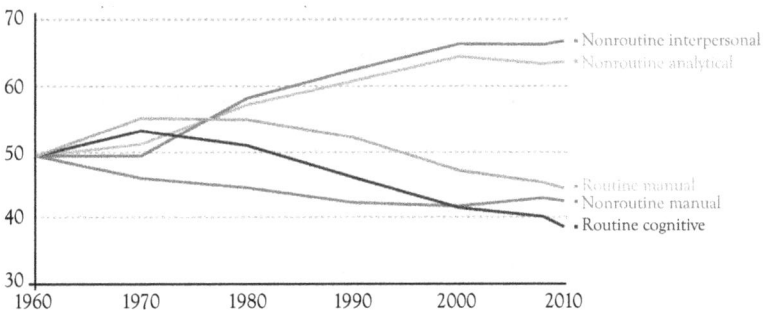

Figure 6.1 The labor market increasingly demands higher-order skills

Source: (World Economic Forum n.d.) Adapted from Levy, Frank and Richard J. Murnane. Third Way NEXT. 2013.

capacity for adaptability, and so on. The World Economic Forum has split in three blocks the competencies that will be needed to succeed in the 21st century (see figure 6.2): foundational literacies, competencies for complex challenges, and character qualities. More importantly, lifelong learning has become a prerequisite for creating a sustainable career.

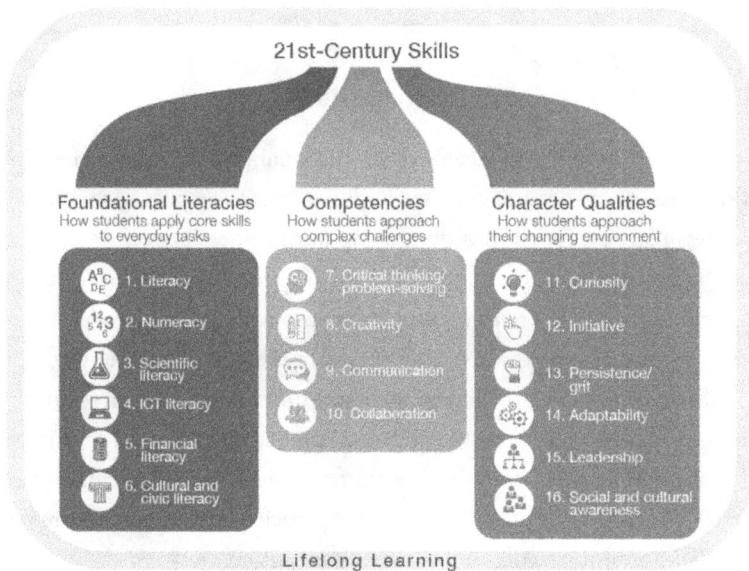

21st-Century Skills

Foundational Literacies	Competencies	Character Qualities
How students apply core skills to everyday tasks	How students approach complex challenges	How students approach their changing environment
1. Literacy	7. Critical thinking/ problem-solving	11. Curiosity
2. Numeracy	8. Creativity	12. Initiative
3. Scientific literacy	9. Communication	13. Persistence/ grit
4. ICT literacy	10. Collaboration	14. Adaptability
5. Financial literacy		15. Leadership
6. Cultural and civic literacy		16. Social and cultural awareness

Lifelong Learning

Figure 6.2 Students require 16 skills for the 21st century

Source: (World Economic Forum n.d.)

This demand for new skills and competences constitutes the big picture of our career's plans. As we move forward in the specifics of our plans, we need to keep in mind that we live and work in a dynamic and global market where the level of skills demanded is substantially different from the one required to the previous generations.

Skills and Competencies

For the sake of this workbook, we will distinguish skills from competencies. We consider skills as "specific intellectual and nonintellectual aptitudes that the individual commands at an average or above average level for example, programming skills, quantitative skills, general knowledge etc."

Competencies are "observable, habitual behaviors that lead to success in a function or task" (Rajadhyaksha 2005).

The crucial difference between skills and competencies is that skills imply an aptitude that distinguishes us individually from other people. A competence is the aptitude that allows us to leverage our role within a team or an organization, for example, command of English language is a skill, but *properly communicating in English* is a competence. Someone could be very good at speaking English, but it does not mean they are good at communicating the message they want in English. Communication implies understanding the receiver's background, knowing how to manage the so-called *noises* of communication, willingness, and attitude to code the message.

In the current context of increasing globalization and complexity, companies prefer more the capacity to work with others rather than individually; therefore, they appreciate more competencies than skills. Furthermore, as we move up on the ladder of our careers, our skills become less relevant than our competences because our responsibilities are more focused on conducting people, business units, and projects. Later in the workbook, we will offer lists of competences and will help you define them for your case.

Exercise—Do You Need to Boost Your Competencies?

A successful development of competencies requires a certain level of our skills. As said before, knowing English does not mean that you can communicate in English. However, you need to have an acceptable level of English before you start working with it.

But beyond skills, you need something we call *attitude* or *character*. Skills *injected* by character become competences. In simple terms, character or attitude is the capacity to exercise our skills in the right way, at the right time, with the right people. We want you now to briefly reflect on your character to have an initial insight on your level of competencies. Observe the following chart (see table 6.1):

Table 6.1 Balance of action thinking, feeling, accessing others

	Action without	*Thinking without*	*Feeling without*	*Accessing others without*
Action		Procrastination	Paralysis	Talk the issue to death
Thinking	May not have the vital information. May not extract all the learning from the consequences of action. May repeat actions not successful in the past.		Over-respond to emotional aspects without the calming influence of reason or past successes.	Lose the information that resides within formal sources or within one's self.
Feeling	Ignore or deny feelings and slip into habitual responses.	Intellectualize, rationalize, to avoid the task.		Lack candor in their feedback
Accessing others	Reinvent the wheel, no support, may offend.	Miss the knowledge and support of others. The benefit of others to push, challenge one's thinking.	Unnecessary isolation.	

Source: Author from (Fullan 2013)

Is any of those behaviors present in your life? If you are a doer, you will act many times without considering other people's interests. If you tend to think over many times what you are supposed to do, it is likely that you will be testing continuously the patience of other people and the limits of your projects.

Any disbalance between thinking or acting or feeling or accessing others will limit your capacity to use your skills in the context of a team or an organization. In Chapter 10, we will work about character development that is the single most important factor that guarantees the exercise of skills, keeping the balance between thinking, acting, feeling, and accessing others.

Your Career at a Glance—An Exercise

We want you to take a look at your career till this point and understand how the context has influenced it. The future is more important than the past, but the latter offers lessons. We will do it through a very simple exercise that has been adapted from one created by IESE Business School.

1. *You are asked to draw a general mapping of your life and career. To do that, you need to:*

   a. *Split the career in equal parts between 4–6 quarters or stages (depending on how long your career has been).*

   b. *In each stage, indicate the 1–2 personal and professional positive and negative top highlights. Indicate only the ones you consider memorable or determinant.*

2. *You must indicate the general, personal, and professional levels of satisfaction on a scale from 1–10 (1 being "not satisfied," 4 "fairly satisfied," 10 "completely fulfilled").*

3. *Then, we suggest you map it using X-axis stages of the career and Y-axis for the level of satisfaction in each stage. The following graph is an example of how it could look like, but you can use your creativity!*

   Part of Exercise—Example "Your career at a glance"

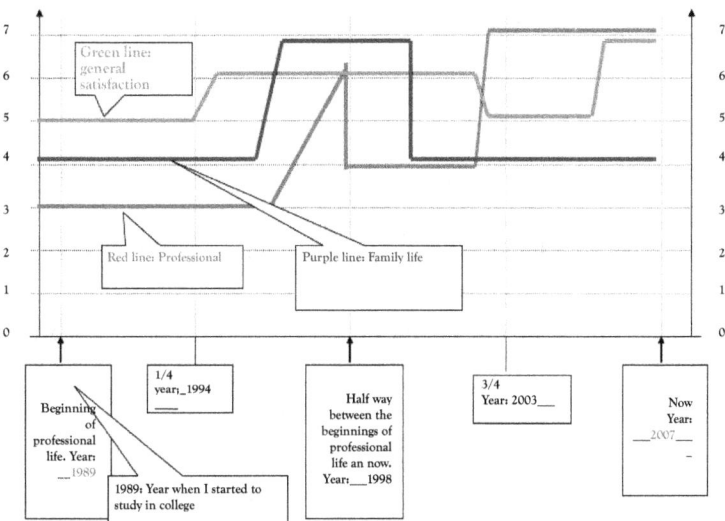

4. *Before moving forward, take some time to reflect on your career. How much do you feel the context has impacted your decisions? How far your career has contributed to your level of personal satisfaction? In which extent, your life and career support or hinder each other?*

_____

_____

_____

_____

_____

_____

Now, please turn to the next exercise in your personal and career journey *"Leader's Journal" and fill in your roadmap—2.1. Retro analysis (based on IESE test).*

The Impact of the Corporate Context

Our experience indicates that many times, the general level of satisfaction does not correlate with the peak of our careers. The unfortunate most common situation is simply *too much work, too little family*. This *imbalance* does not work well, even from a business perspective, as we know that managers who are not satisfied with life will end up losing satisfaction in career as well.

In order to work on this, IESE business school has created an index to study how businesses are doing regarding family–work balance, the IFREI (IESE Family Responsible Employer Index). It looks at policies, facilitators, culture, and results. At the end of the study, it classifies businesses in four groups according to how they make it easy for family–work balance:

A. Enriching: Environment that systematically facilitates work–family balance
B. Positive: Environment that occasionally facilitates work–family balance
C. Difficult: Environment that occasionally hinders work–family balance
D. Contaminating: Environment that systematically hinders work–family balance

In the global study (2012), almost half of the businesses are in the C group, whereas only one of each 10 businesses are in the A group. These are the numbers for the global study:

A. World: 10 percent
B. World: 29 percent
C. World 49 percent
D. World 12 percent

Of course, in order to have a healthy personal and career development, it is crucial to find ways to balance work and family life and to find the appropriate corporate context. If you look at your career or life map from the previous section, you might find out that some of the moments where general satisfaction was low were correlated with a work environment leaning toward C to D levels. It is certainly very challenging for a manager to have an acceptable level of career and life satisfaction if the environment where he or she operates is neither enriching nor supportive.

Conclusions—Avoiding the Risk of Social Conditioning

The context is a fundamental element of our life or career development. We are social creatures and, therefore, we tend to accommodate to the context and to the people who are around us—to act in a way the society and peer groups approve. Though we need alignment with the context, a pure attitude of *social conformity* will hinder our capacity for leadership and for use of our potential life.

In this chapter, we have stated the difference between skills and competencies. Our character determines our level of competencies. Skills make us effective as individual contributors; competencies make our skills valid in the context of teams and organizations. Competencies are built upon the skills, so it means that competencies do not substitute skills, and in a certain way, they are skills put in action in team settings.

The corporate context and our workload impact our level of career and life satisfaction. We have *taken a flashback picture* of our career or life development in order to start planning the future.

CHAPTER 7

Assessment of Context and Competencies II

Introduction

Chapter 6 introduced the relevance of the context (aka market) and helped you to understand the big picture of your career and the linkages between context and career. This chapter will focus on your current context in order for you to decide the next short- and long-term decisions in terms of career choices and the development of competencies.

It is important at this point to consider the role of transitions as the context of the 21st century is one of continuous changes. We live in an era of short business and career cycles, which triggers that we see changes in our professional settings much more often than in the past.

Dancing With Transitions

According to Dr. Rivera, a transition or crisis is a radical change in the context. It could be positive (like promotion) or negative (losing your job). In any case, a radical change implies challenges to expected outcomes and needed competences.

As our careers evolve, we go through different transitions or crises. We generally start our careers and progress based on the skills we and others perceive as strengths. The challenge is that, as we use our skills and receive *prizes* for that, our development needs remain generally hidden. That is the reason why career experts indicate that our strengths are the reverse mirror of our development needs.

In the past, human resource (HR) specialists would help us slowly assess our future development needs and approach a plan for them. The challenge today, as has been said earlier, is that the transitions and crises appear more often without giving us really time for adaptation. A contemporary phenomenon appears then that is called *derailment*: crashing as we move fast-speed in our careers (like fast-speed trains derailing).

Our focus today is to prevent derailment, detecting the derailment risks we confront. Derailment risk is when a strength becomes the main risk factor for our long-term development, for example, a philologist that is proofreading texts in a language generally will become very inflexible with processes and with people.

According to the Stanford Graduate School of Business, the different transitions we face early in our careers are the following (see table 7.1):

Table 7.1 Types of personal and career transitions

Type	Role transitions	Business transitions	Personal transitions
Characteristic challenges	• From individual contributor to first-time manager • Taking responsibility for team performance • Dealing with difficult subordinates • Motivating others (who are not like you)	• Starting something new • Managing growth • Turning around a group or business • Taking a team or business to the next level • Leading across cultures	• Managing strategic differences with a boss or peer • Navigating and correcting ethically questionable practices • Blending work, life, and family • Dealing with professional setbacks

Source: Handouts of program Leadership in Focus (Stanford Graduate School of Business 2012)

Observing the participants of our programs, we perceive that in reality, these transitions appear together more and more often. For example, those in role or business transitions face generally personal transitions consequently. This is particularly apparent in those people engaged in the start-up community, as their careers become volatile.

Furthermore, transitions imply not only different sets of skills but also a different mindset. The mindset or what the classics call *forma mentis* is probably the most difficult side to change. The mindset is built by our personality and values, as we have discussed in the first part of the book. As we have seen, we can modulate our personality and values, but that takes a long time.

A question arises then: is it possible to quickly get adapted to new transitions? Is the traditional career or competencies fit model still valid?

In the past, we have taught that career or competencies fit is essential when a person starts working in a new position and when they have a transition (personal > business > role transition). Depending on the new positions, the competencies that are required are different, and we are not always ready to respond to the new challenges. However, looking at the present time of continuous changes and transitions, we are not sure this aspiration of finding the right person for the right job is still valid. We will leave this dilemma for other publications.

Core Exercise—SWOT Analysis
of Our Current Career

The first thing we are going to do is a SWOT analysis for the career. Based on this SWOT, we will define short-term goals and priorities to implement them. A tool called the Action Contract will be used later for describing and making actionable these goals. We believe you have already encountered in some way or other SWOT as a tool for strategic planning. We are applying the same methodology, though adapted to the problem of career. We suggest you do the next exercise slowly—three hours is a good benchmark—and consider all the issues we have dealt with so far. A preparatory reading of the parts you have already filled in the roadmap is advisable.

Your Career's SWOT (Strengths, Weaknesses, Opportunities, and Threats)

Please be advised that the following questions are guiding questions. It means that you could and should explore other issues that you feel could help you complete your SWOT better. At the end of the exercise, you must feel that you are very realistic and sincere with yourself. As with other tests, we suggest you show your findings to people who know you well.

1. *Strengths: Knowing and using your powers can make you happier and more fulfilled at work.*
   Questions to consider
   What competitive advantages do you possess that others do not have (e.g., skills or competencies, certifications, education, or connections)?
   What do you do better than others do?
   What personal and professional resources do you have?
   What do others (and especially your supervisor) see as your strengths?
   Which of your achievements are you most proud of?
   Are you part of a unique network? If so, what influential connections do you have?
   Observing my current strengths, which of them could become a derailment risk?

   _____

   _____

   _____

_____

_____

_____

_____

_____

_____

_____

_____

_____

_____

_____

_____

_____

2. *Weaknesses: Be realistic—it is best to know (and accept) your flaws.*
   Questions to consider
   In which tasks or situations you do not feel confident.
   What do the people around you consider as your weaknesses?
   Which is the weakest side of your education and skills training?
   What are your negative work habits (e.g., are you often late, are you dis-
   organized, do you have a short temper, or are you poor at handling stress)?

_____

_____

_____

_____

_____

_____

_____

_____

_____

_____

_____

_____

_____

3. *Opportunities: Look closely at your strengths and weaknesses, they might offer some opportunities.*

   Questions to consider

   Are there any new technologies (i.e., social media) that can help you?

   Is your industry growing, and what can you gain from that?

   How can your network of people come in handy?

   Which are the weaknesses of your competitors?

   Are there any windows of opportunity in your company or industry?

   What is the negative feedback from your customers or vendors about something in your company? Can you fix it?

   _____

   _____

   _____

   _____

   _____

   _____

   _____

   _____

   _____

   _____

4. *Threats: Highlighting the problems, so you could find the solutions.*

   Questions to consider

   Are there any obstacles you currently face, or you could face in the foreseeable future?

   Is the environment over-competitive?

   Is your position threatened by technology?

   Could any of your weaknesses lead to threats?

   _____

   _____

   _____

_____

_____

_____

_____

_____

_____

_____

_____

_____

_____

_____

_____

_____

_____

Now, please turn to the exercise in your personal and career journey Leader's Journal and fill in your roadmap—2.2 My current career 2.2.1 General questions about your current position

Conclusions

In this chapter, we have analyzed our current context considering the era of continuous transitions where we are in. Transitions are radical changes that happen at a personal or a professional level, and they could seriously compromise our professional and personal health, and they could become big opportunities for development.

Adaptability to change has long been named as one of the key competences for the future. It makes sense as we can damage our careers if we just try to keep doing the same every time the context changes, or if we do not know how to quickly harmonize with the new teams or organizations we are sent in, or we focus too much on the tasks and have difficulties to build new relationships.

Transitions or crises imply that we might have to start over again frequently. Hence, those strengths that have sustained our careers in the previous phases might not be so appreciated anymore, and they might have even hindered the awareness and development of other competencies. In a nutshell, our strengths might be our derailment risks. Hence, the ability to systematically diagnose our real status and learn become the key for success in the long run.

CHAPTER 8

Competencies Development Plan

Introduction: the Attitude of Your Company Matters

Having defined in the previous chapter our position in the market and knowing our career–life goals (in previous chapters), we are in a condition to specifically decide the competencies we want to develop and the plan for that. We will create a *competencies development plan* for the short and long run.

The best methodology for developing competencies is *on-the-job learning*. Prof. Chinchilla says, "and it is true that by managing competencies professionally, a company can become a school of habits" (Nuria and Maruja 2013). This is the reason why the best personal leadership programs are project-based and generally intertwined with the position and responsibilities we have in the corporate setting.

Though companies are more focused on short-term skills development, the best way to keep and develop talent is to provide the capacity for training the long-term competencies of the employees. As difficult as it sounds. Every company and every career stage can become a real school of habits or competencies.

In a company that is focused on the *jobs* that should be done, the management will largely concentrate on commanding specific *tasks* of the employees. In this context, the maximum an employee could achieve is sustaining his or her *career* through avoidance of mistakes but without ambitions in terms of growth. When employees are focused on tasks and are driven by command aimed at sustaining their positions, then they become very much context-dependent. The reason is that they are prevented from thinking strategically about their jobs and competencies.

Second, if a company tries to help employees to build careers around jobs—and not just simply comply with objectives—managers will create corporate environments that support more synergies between the personal goals of the employees and the corporate needs. In this case, employees have more chances not only of sustaining their jobs, but also of creating the habit of thinking career-wise. If employees focus on objectives, the company encourages their proactivity and result orientation.

Third, if a company seeks to instill in employees and managers a vision around their careers and jobs, managers will also encourage the proactivity of the employees through reflection of the linkages between the company's goals and their professional–personal anchors. For this purpose, they will likely use coaching as a regular tool for management. Employees can expect in this context to be transformed in those stages and jobs where they work. Hence, they become less context-dependent, as they have been acquiring competencies, which make them flexible to perform through transitions.

If a manager takes a paternalistic role and instructs people all the time, as generally happens in companies focusing on tasks, employees never become independent, neither the company nor of the context. By contrast, if managers focus on coaching and developing the people, they become less dependent on the company and the context.

Your Development Potential and the Action Contract

Once we have discussed at length in the previous chapters and in the introduction to this chapter the impact of context on our personal development, it is time to define a plan. But, before that, we want you to be clear that even though the corporate environment and the market reality are very influential, you still have a fair amount of personal responsibility for your own growth.

One of the most traditional formulas of job performance is the following:

> *Job Performance* = Attitude (willingness to perform) × Aptitude (capacity to perform) × Corporate support (company culture, systems, management style, etc.)

We can apply this formula to your *personal development performance* or *individual potential growth* as well.

Personal development performance = Attitude (willingness to grow)
× Aptitude (skills and previous background) × Corporate support

Your attitude will depend directly from your vision, values, and how far you see the relevance of the growth. Managers can mainly influence the later, that is, explaining the impact of growth on the financial conditions of the work contract. Aptitude depends on your previous background. The responsibility of the managers here is largely constraint to a proper recruitment process. Corporate support depends on whether the company wants to focus on the compliance of employees to specific jobs or rather foster the proactivity of the employees in building their careers, as has been explained in the introduction.

In order to set up a clear plan for your personal development, we will offer a specific tool we have been working with for years: action plan contract. Though it looks very simple, it will require reflection, time for preparation, and feedback from your coaches or people you rely upon.

The action plan contract follows the same principles that other *coaching practices* as delegating the ownership of the decision to the coachee and keeping the long-term picture actionable with specific short-term goals. We will come back to coaching at the end of the workbook. These techniques are very useful because they test your willingness to change (attitude in the formula of personal development performance), as you are required to be very specific on the what and the how of your improvement process.

Action Plan Contract—An Exercise

Action contract is a tool that we use in order to be very specific about the development plan of the participants. The key characteristics of the action contract is that it defines the specific competencies that we want to develop, how it would be developed, and the so-called SMART[1] objectives for that development. Even though you have only two questions, we suggest you take between two and three hours to complete its first draft.

Based on your SWOT analysis, the long-term vision you set up for yourself in Chapter 5, and the results of the kaleidoscope strategy, which is your next career goal (for the next 1–2 years)? Please, give reasons.

For example: promotion to a new position, launching a start-up, and so forth.

Which are the 1–2 competencies you realistically think you need to focus on and develop during the next 1–2 years? Please, give reasons.

For example: Team orientation because I am defensive in my dealings with my teammates, besides I do not know how to listen. Further, I am expected to be offered a position where my main responsibilities will be related to team management.

_____

_____

_____

Please, specify 1–2 objectives for each of the competencies or skills you think you should develop. Please, use SMART principles to define your objectives for example (given that the competence is team orientation): I will answer to my teammates' phone calls promptly and pleasantly. I will ask those mates how they feel when they call me. I would like to have a substantial improvement by the end of the project where I am involved.

_____

_____

---

[1]   Specific (simple, sensible, significant).
Measurable (meaningful, motivating).
Achievable (agreed, attainable).
Relevant (reasonable, realistic and resourced, results-based).
Time bound (time-based, time limited, time or cost limited, timely, time-sensitive).

_____

_____

_____

_____

_____

_____

Now, please turn to the next exercise in your personal and career journey "Leader's Journal" and fill in your roadmap—2.2.2. Assessment of my short-term competencies' development needs and 2.2.3. Action Contract and the conclusions from this exercise.

Tips for Learning—List of Competencies and the Relevance of Innovation Skills

It is good to choose a list of competencies that can help us fulfill the action plan contract. There are numerous lists of competencies that are applicable in business contexts. They are generally categorized in different ways, but all of them include three types of competencies—technical skills, personality, and business competencies. We offer next a list of competencies (see table 8.1) by Cardona and Lombardía (2005), but this list is purely indicative!

Table 8.1 Fundamental managerial competencies

Business dimension	**Interpersonal dimension**	**Personal dimension**
Business vision	Communication	Initiative
Organizational vision	Conflict management	Optimism
Resource management	Charisma	Ambition
Customer orientation	Delegation	Time management
Networking	Coaching	Information management
Negotiation	Teamwork	Stress management

Source: (García-Lombardía and Cardona 2005)

In the short run, innovation competences are the key. These skills are particularly relevant to taking advantage of the opportunities that appear often, quickly, and radically during the so-called Fourth Industrial Revolution. This is particularly true as stable jobs are part of the pasts and

companies to become an innovation ecosystem. In figure 8.1 following below, you can see the outlining of these competencies by Prof. Gregersen and Christensen of Stanford.

The innovator's DNA model for generating innovative ideas

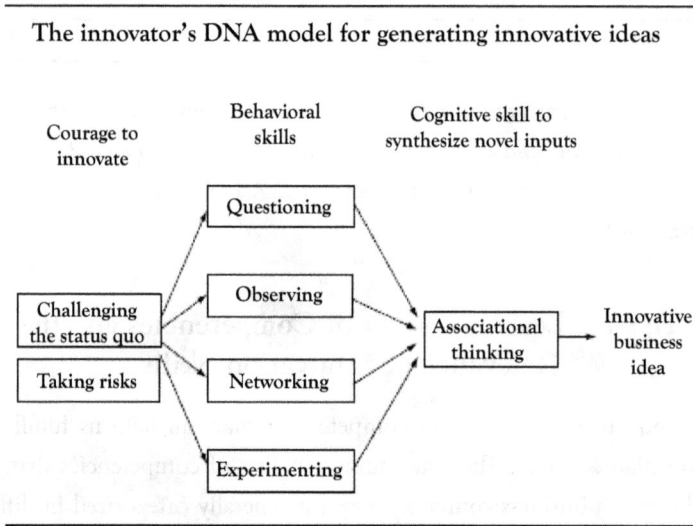

Figure 8.1 The innovator's DNA model for generating innovative ideas

Source: (Dyer, Gregersen and Christensen 2011)

The core competence for innovating is the cognitive skill of associational thinking. The reason why some people are better at generating associations than others is due to the way their brains work, how they have been educated, and the variety of experiences to which they are generally exposed. However, a more critical reason is that they engage more frequently in the behavioral skills of questioning, observing, networking, and experimenting—these operate as motivators for associational thinking. Another key element is the courage to innovate, meaning they are willing to embrace a mission of change and take the risks to make change happen. If a person wants to be good at it, they need to practice generating ideas as well as engage in questioning, observing, networking, and experimenting. A. G. Lafley declared "innovation is the central job of every leader—business unit managers, functional leaders, and the CEO" (Dyer, Gregersen and Christensen 2011).

The Artifact: An Illustration of How Companies Could Become Schools of Competencies—An Exercise

This exercise, designed by Prof. Rivera, is intended to simulate how companies could develop their people meanwhile they push for short-term results. Let us be honest: the enormous pressure managers impose on employees in terms of short-term performance is one of the most important obstacles for employees' development. Paradoxically, the organizations, which should have the main interest on developing competences many times, become the main blockers. The artifact exercise aims to offer a realistic view on how people could develop themselves despite the context and making use of the context.

Companies can develop their people if they identify realistically their potential contribution and if they set up mini development plans using projects as sort of competences labs.

This is a group task and must be implemented in such a setting (5 to 10 people). Ideally, you will compete with other or other groups. If you do not have peers to work with, the task may be skipped, but it is advised that you fill all the tasks to experience the workbook fully.

Part I: Choosing the Challenge

Choose a very difficult challenge for the group (e.g., create the most extraordinary and unforgettable outdoor experience for executives and employees of your company. The company should be in agreement!).

Part II: Designing the Implementation of the Challenge

- *Brainstorming: 10 minutes NB! During brainstorming, it is not allowed: criticize ideas and deliver negative comments. Write down all ideas.*
- *Vote the best. five minutes.*
- *Prepare an elevator pitch of up to two minutes. 10 minutes.*
- *Send the elevator pitch to the other groups (by written). Feedback from the other groups with suggestion(s) or comment(s) (by written). 15 minutes.*

- If you have time, compare the idea with existing products or services.
- Prepare the final version of the elevator pitch. 10 minutes.

Part III: Picking Responsibilities and Competencies

- The member, who proposed the idea, becomes the group's leader and facilitator.
- List the top 10 contributions needed for implementing successfully the idea. 15 minutes.
- Create a list of many common skills or qualities that members of the group have in common (except the leader). Avoid writing things that are immediately obvious. 10 minutes.
- Record unique skills and qualities; meaning, items that only apply to one person in the group.
- Please, find at least two unique qualities and strengths per person (except the leader). 10 minutes.
- Distribute the contributions between the group's members according to their skills and qualities. 10 minutes.

Part IV: Action Plan Contract

Every member will fill the action plan contract of competencies that want to develop during the implementation of the project. Leader will assist every member in the process and sign the contract. 60 minutes.

Important Notes:
It is important to respect the sequence of the steps.
Participants of this exercise should feel a safe environment.
The time allocated for the tasks should be respected.

In a way, this activity is like a serious game—gamification of the context of competence development. Imagine if the company implements this sort of dynamics for every project that it undertakes. In this way, it could become a school of competencies combining short-term goals with long-term objectives in terms of competencies.

Conclusions

As we can see in this chapter, competencies development requires long-term thinking and the organization's attitude to provide the right context. Employees need a context that fosters strategic thinking, synergy, and coaching if they are willing to equip themselves not only with technical skills to properly execute tasks but also with long-term business and technical competencies.

Learning competencies requires the right attitude also of the individuals that is proven in the decision to commit to very specific and measurable goals. We have suggested designing these goals using the tool of the action plan contract.

Finally, the learning of each competence by adults is better done in project-based settings where the employees can have an appropriate context for practice and can better perceive the importance of their improvement.

Your roadmap now starts to look quite full. From describing your personality till a very specific definition of the competencies you want to develop in order to move forward. We suggest you read again all that you have written, then you can better understand the value of what is coming next.

CHAPTER 9

Transition, Failure, Resilience

Introduction

Eisenhower once said, "planning is everything, plan is nothing." There is some sense in this sentence, especially in the current context of high turbulence with different industrial sectors converging and technologies disrupting the operations of companies. We have discussed at length in the previous chapters the era of transitions we are in and how to plan the development of our competences to succeed. But, what if we fail? This is the question we will be dealing with in this chapter.

Failure has always been part of any project, career, and business. The difference now is the potential frequency of failures. As the occurrence of transitions has increased, the same happens with failures, as a transition is, by definition, a very risky context due to its characteristic of *radical change*.

In this chapter, we will elaborate on the key risks each type of transition generates, how do we learn from previous failures, how do we get over future derailments, how do we work with ourselves if failure appears, and how do we plan our short-term objectives after failing. A key competence we will exercise during the *failing process* is resilience; therefore, it will appear several times during the chapter.

Leadership Pipeline, Transitions' Cycle, and Resilience

If we look at the job market in the 1970s and 1980s, we could see that there has been much more stability than in the previous decades. People used to have longer careers in different corporations and professions. This is the reason why transition and resilience have become essential parts in any personal development program.

We have traditionally been talking about the so-called leadership pipeline that represented the changes in responsibility every individual was facing sequentially during their time at a company. The first step was usually as an individual performer, second as manager of other people or small teams of people, then managers of other managers, and the pipeline continues all the way to general manager.

This leadership pipeline used to take a relatively long period of time depending on the sector and the company, and the people had years to get ready for the next step. Though careers today face quicker changes, as we have repeatedly said, and tenure in one specific company might be shorter, the essentials of the leadership pipeline remain. Even freelancers, who are the ultimate individualistic performers, if they succeed, they end up creating their own team, startups, and a small company and then, the leadership pipeline starts. The difference between the current and the past pipelines is that the hierarchical structures have become more elastic and, in some cases, diffused.

The moral is that even in a context of continuous changes and predominance of careers outside large and hierarchical corporations, people end up facing a sort of leadership pipeline with all the consequences in terms of recognition, compensation, and responsibility.

As in any change process, the psychological resistance used to be the main barrier. Resistance to change is the consequence of our desire to stay in our comfort zone. We call it the *wall of fear*—the resistance to change in career development. The root of the wall of fear is both the rational recognition of my comfort zone and the irrational emotions in front of something that is uncertain. This is the reason why in order to cross it, we need both rational guidance and emotional support.

Coaching is a tool we will touch upon briefly in Chapter 11. Generally, it is one of the most recommended instruments, as it helps to have mental clarity and emotional support. As most individuals cannot afford the cost of professional coaching, companies should start looking at making coaching part of the benefits they offer to their employees.

Any transition generates fear. If we do not cross it or if we do it through the wrong side, we fail. Sometimes, we even cross it, but we derail as we try to continue behaving as we did in previous positions without the awareness that our context had changed.

Identifying Our Derailment Risks—An Exercise

Over time, our success as a leader will depend less on our individual skills and more on our ability to lead others. Unfortunately, leadership is one of the competences most individuals lack when they land in corporate careers.

Generally, our careers go at a fast speed, and the speed is propelled by our strengths. However, as the level of responsibility increases and our leadership impact unfolds, our strengths become metaphorically like the engine of a larger vehicle—a train! It means that those things that keep us on the direction, meaning the rails, at some level of speed might not be able to hold anymore. This is called the phenomenon of a derailment (see figure 9.1).

Figure 9.1 Train derailment

Source: (Akta 2018)

You can see next some examples of derailment found among professional managers that lead them to failure in their transitions:

1. *People that have been perfectionists on their own tasks. This capacity to make things till the end and without mistakes might become a bottleneck for an organization once they become managers as they tend to be perfectionists not only with their own tasks, but also with responsibilities*
2. *People who are hard workers and are ready to go the extra mile in every activity they take; they could easily fall into burnout once the level of responsibilities substantially increases*

3. *People who used to be very creative and who can find new angles and visions for everything they undertake; they might create organizations without the necessary structure*

4. *People who are extremely result-oriented might be too harsh with their team members, which can really make it difficult their capacity to create organizations around their responsibilities.*

These are only a few examples of derailment risks. Identifying this risk early in career and cultivating honesty can help to overcome the wall of fear when the needs of transitions appear.

Now, please turn to the exercise in your personal and career journey Leader's Journal and start filling in your roadmap the derailment risks table.

Action Plan Contract—An Exercise

This action contract is similar in format to the previous chapter, now applied to a transition, so get ready for it.

1. *Based upon our discussion on transitions and derailment risks, which are the 2–3 competencies you realistically think you need to focus to get ready for the next transition? Please, give reasons. For example: customer orientation because there will be a substantial increase of competition.*

   _____

   _____

   _____

   _____

   _____

   _____

   _____

   _____

2. *Please, specify 1–2 SMART objectives for each of the competencies you should develop.*
   For example: answer customers' phone calls promptly and pleasantly.

   _____

   _____

   _____

   _____

   _____

   _____

   _____

   _____

Failure and Resilience

"The most important thing to learn right now is to learn from failure. You will fail. Failure is essential for success," John Riccitiello, CEO of Electronic Arts (Bryant 2011). Failure is part of success. It is something we have to know, and our competence development plan has to include resilience.

A good example is sport, which will help us introduce the need to grow in resilience. If we look at elite athletes, we will realize that they all have failed. That is the reason why we should try to emulate their competences in this regard. According to the research on recovery in sports, there are mainly two extrinsic motivational factors that help athletes to manage failure: the support of a coach and the social circle.

Researchers have also found up to seven motivational strategies that are useful in downturns among sportsmen: setting small goals or outperforming yourself, self-talk, setting priorities, keeping positive perception, self-observing, self-analyses and learning, and perceiving failures as a normal part of the process.

What is resilience? We define resilience as the capacity to avoid adverse mental and physical outcomes following exposure to failure or extreme stress.

There are, in fact, three potential dimensions of a response to resilience:

- Perspective: Once the failure has occurred, you have to get self-distance, realism, and acceptance.
- Search for meaning: It includes things such as looking deeper at what happens, observing an event in the framework of the big picture, focusing your objectives, and rebuilding what is necessary.
- Resources: When a failure occurs, we need to take factual stock of all the resources we have available in order to deal with it. We should care for all of them: physical resources, mental resources, personal competencies, and social relationships.

However, how to build resilience? Resilience is a competence, and, as so, it needs to be practiced. This competence allows us, in case of failure, to get the right perspective, to search for meaning, and to enlist the resources for proper decision making.

CV of Failures—An Exercise

Part of the training in resilience implies a certain familiarization to failure. In simple terms, we need to develop the skin to get along with the emotional drama that comes along with the term failure. One way is to recognize those failures we had in our life, even though we have forgotten about them. The following exercise will help you with this.

Write a resume of failures, meaning those things that we have tried, but we have not achieved. Some organizations working in entrepreneurship used to require their participants to provide a record of the things their startups failed to do because it indicates the resilience, commitment to the project, and the learning capacity for the future. We offer to our students that they actually create the CV of failures. The task is very simple; they have to record failures in different areas of their professional careers. An example is provided as follows (see figure 9.2):

SAM'S CV OF FAILURES

This is my CV of Failures. For more info. see: http://dx.doi.org/10.1038/nj7322-467a
My real CV (with my actually accomplishments) can be found
here: http://everydayscientist.com/CV/sjl_CV.pdf

SCHOOLS I WAS REJECTED FROM

Berkeley rejected me for grad school	2004
I withdrew my undergrad application for Stanford	2001

POSITIONS I FAILED TO GET

Not accepted to summer research program at the Jackson Laboratory	2000

AWARDS, FELLOWSHIPS & GRANTS REJECTED

NIH NRSA postdoctoral fellowship indefinitely unfunded	2010
DOD postdoctoral fellowship not recommended for funding	2010
Miller Fellowship rejected	2010
ACS Younger Chemist Leadership Development Award rejected	2010
NSF Graduate Research Fellowship rejected again	2005
DOD NDSEG application rejected	2004
NSF Graduate Research Fellowship rejected	2004
Hertz Fellowship application rejected	2004

MANUSCRIPTS REJECTED

Angew. Chem. rejected my manuscript	2009

Figure 9.2 Sam's CV of failures

Source: (Every Day Scientist)

Designing the Critical Event Review

A very effective tool we use in class in order to understand how to learn from failure, but also in general from any event is the so-called critical event review (CER). It is a highly structured essay-type assignment where the reader has to reply to open-ended questions. These questions have the following objectives:

1. Take stock of the different circumstances that surrounded the specific event
2. Analyze the different emotional and nonemotional reactions of the individual phasing the event
3. To think about what was missing in their reactions in order to deal better with similar events in the future
4. To conclude specific objectives for future events

The CER is a very powerful tool because it allows the individual to have more perspective of the event as he or she is self-distancing from it. He or she is taking a realistic perspective upon it, and he or she is embracing both the event and his or her reactions.

Critical Event Review—An Exercise

Please, create a CER of a failure you remember.

A CER should be between 200 and 500 words long; although you may find that you sometimes want to make them longer. The purpose of a CER is to focus on a specific experience and mine it for leadership lessons.

Structure of Each CER

The following framework provides the structure with which to reflect on the specific incident or experience.
Questions to consider

1. *When*

2. *Setting*

3. *Who did I engage with? What happened?*

_____

_____

_____

_____

_____

_____

4. *What did I do and say?*

_____

_____

_____

_____

_____

_____

_____

5. *How could others perceive it?*

_____

_____

_____

_____

_____

_____

_____

6. *How did I feel?*

_____

_____

_____

_____

_____

_____

_____

7. *What was I thinking?*

_____

_____

_____

_____

_____

_____

_____

_____

8. *What was the issue I was trying to address?*

_____

_____

_____

_____

_____

_____

_____

9. *What did it remind me of? (Which previous experiences does it remind me of?)*

_____

_____

_____

_____

_____

_____

_____

10. *What could I have done and said differently?*

_____

_____

_____

_____

_____

_____

_____

_____

_____

11. *What did I notice during this experience—thoughts, feelings, body symptoms, and so on?*

_____

_____

_____

_____

_____

_____

12. *What am I resisting?*

_____

_____

_____

_____

_____

13. *What is new, unfamiliar, or unpleasant?*

_____

_____

_____

_____

_____

_____

14. *How do I hold others accountable for how I am feeling?*

_____

_____

_____

_____

_____

_____

_____

15. *What are the lessons in this for me?*

_____

_____

_____

_____

_____

_____

_____

_____

_____

_____

_____

_____

_____

_____

_____

Conclusions

You can juggle a lot more balls if you recognize that some balls are made of rubber and others are made of glass. Rubber balls bounce. Glass balls shatter. You can drop the rubber balls and usually recover easily enough. Drop a glass ball and you're likely done with that one (Eblin 2017).

In this chapter, we have seen that transition and failure will be constant phenomenon in our careers and will eventually lead us to rethink our leadership capacities and will challenge our resilience. We also saw very specific tools in order to reflect on the different events surrounding transition and failure, and we have explained the needs of reviewing our derailment risks. There are three very strong potential derailers that we have to seriously avoid:

(1) Blaming others of our failures, taking the role of a victim
(2) Letting our emotions to take over the whole of our reaction, the CER tool that we have indicated in this chapter is a good instrument to prepare us for the future failures based on our past experiences
(3) Our lack of realism toward our experience that prevents many people from actually learning from their experience, and that could happen partially because sometimes we do not stop to look at what we have done and sometimes because our wall of fear is preventing us from going beyond our limitations

PART III

Ownership of Your Daily Agenda

CHAPTER 10

Life Balance and Time Management

Introduction

Though the title initially refers to time management, the core of the chapter is emotional intelligence, which is one of the most popular topics in the personal development area since the 1980s.

Time management means essentially the capacity to set up the right order of priorities and, consequently, to put in order our daily agenda. In simple words, it implies to do the right thing, at the right time, and with the right doses.

This is the core of emotional intelligence: the capacity to rationally control our irrational impulses in order to deliver what is right. In our understanding, emotional intelligence as such is a misleading name, as emotional intelligence is broader than the control of our emotions. Therefore, we prefer to call emotional intelligence *character-building*.

After dealing with our life and career objectives in the long and short term, we felt it was important for you to see the impact of these big decisions in the present day. That is why, we include a short third part of the book that helps you live up to your priorities every day. The current chapter deals with the management of your emotions and character in order to keep you on track by yourself every day. The next chapter will deal with coaching, which is a tool you can use to receive the support we all need to keep moving forward on our development.

Emotional Intelligence

Though it seems old-fashioned, virtue—or good habit—is crucial to be a good leader. Daily *virtue in action* is the crucial input of emotional intelligence. It means the capacity to act according to our heart. Heart does not mean only according to our emotions, but according to the right combination of reason and emotions. As the philosopher B. Pascal said, "we arrive at the truth not by reason only, but also by the heart" (Pascal, Rogers, Cousin and Louandre 1861).

Emotional intelligence is a concept that was popularized by D. Goleman in 1998. It refers to "the capacity for recognizing our own feelings and those of others, for motivating ourselves, and for managing emotions well in ourselves and our relationships" (Goleman, 2006). Practically speaking, it is about knowing how you and others feel and what to do about it; knowing what feels good and what feels bad and how to get from bad to good; and possessing the emotional awareness, sensitivity, and the management skills that will help us to maximize our long-term happiness and survival.

During this chapter, we will outline some of the key insights about what emotional intelligence is and how to build it, and we will offer a couple exercises to assess it and practice it.

Summary of Emotional Intelligence

Emotional intelligence is just one type of intelligence among seven identified by Gardner: verbal or linguistic, logical or mathematical, visual or spatial, musical, bodily or kinesthetic, interpersonal, and intrapersonal, according to H. Gardner (Gardner, 2011).

Emotional intelligence is divided principally in two parts:

- Personal competence: It includes self-awareness and self-management.
- Social competence: It is formed by social awareness and relationship management.

Emotional intelligence is an old concept, which is very trendy now. Plato, while describing the real and desired leader, implied already the importance of an appropriate level of emotional intelligence:

A man who combines good memory, readiness to learn, breadth of vision and grace, and be a friend of truth, justice, courage, and self-control. Aren't they the only people to whom you would entrust your state? (Krell 1990)

Emotional intelligence is a practical competence, and for this reason, practice is necessary. If this practical skill is missing, a lack of self-control can happen, and this has enormous repercussions even in our social relationships.

In order to avoid that kind of problems, experts in emotional intelligence suggest to work on self-control mechanisms such as:

- Rules of behavior (I do not do X)
- Precommitment (agreeing to deadlines)
- Rationing (limiting consumption)
- Physical distance (e.g., alarm clock across the room)
- Mental budgeting (e.g., *entertainment budget*)

Character and Virtues

As we said in the introduction, emotional intelligence is what classical authors have called character-building. Character is the combination between the fixed part of our personality (coming from our inheritance and childhood experiences) and the negative and positive habits that we have developed during our lives.

Our personality does not substantially change from our early life onward; however, it can be molded, or it can become a dominant force in our lives. In simple terms, our habits will allow us to dominate our personality in order that we can fulfill our everyday duties properly or, if we have not developed positive habits, our personality will dominate us without us being able to fulfill everyday duties.

This is the reason why W. Bennis said, "Leadership is a metaphor for centeredness, congruity and balance in one's life" (Havard 2007). Someone who wants to have control over his or her own everyday life needs strong character, what essentially means a strong base of virtues that is the right word for *positive habits*. The virtues that the classics suggested are the following (see figure 10.1):

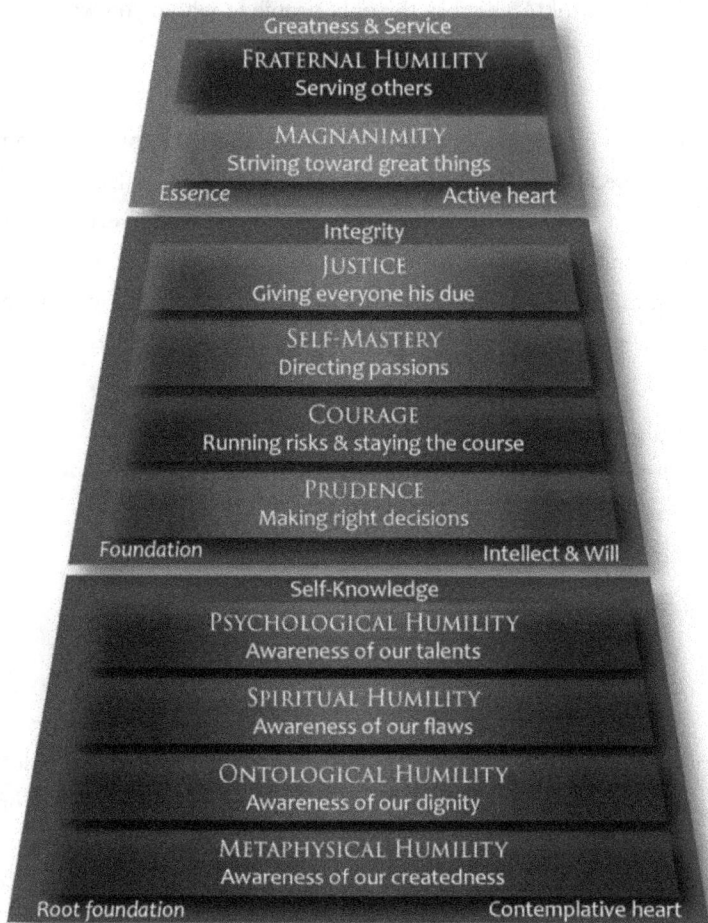

Figure 10.1 Virtuous leadership

Source: (Virtuous Leadership Institute 2017)

The core virtues or cardinal virtues are prudence, courage, self-mastery, and justice. They represent the foundation of the edifice of our character, and they demand, in order to be complete, the virtues of humility and magnanimity. These virtues provide the tutor to modulate our personality and make us behave according to what we consider our right priorities.

In a letter to Lucilius, Seneca would say "It is the spirit that you should change and not the climate. Though you cross the immense ocean, your vices will follow you wherever you go. Why do you wonder that no journeys benefit you, if you always bring yourself with you? What is important is not where you go, but WHO YOU ARE when you go." In the same way that companies could be schools of competences, life is the school of character we need.

Good Character Has Multiple Benefits

First, the virtues allow us to enjoy rewarding and productive lives. So, someone who has what is called solid character has a bigger sense of freedom in their actions. The reason is that they do basically what they want, as they have clarity in the process of decision making (virtue of prudence and magnanimity) but also because they have the strength to deliver what they have decided (virtues of fortitude and self-control).

The second benefit, the more people with good character, the healthier our society. Looking at our families and organizations, we can see that many of the projects that fail and many of the conflicts that arise are due to sloppy work, meaning where it has not been done with proper quality, it has been delayed, or it has not been done at the right time. Even when the process is standard and set, you can never regulate everything that people should do, every action that they should implement. That implies that the planning of processes does not replace the need of character.

Good character-building guarantees quality, at work and it guarantees life standards. Character brings order in life, and order takes care of people. So, when character is present, less remedial actions are needed in all life and professional aspects. Organizations and society need us to be reliable, meaning that we can deliver on what we promised. That is the core of integrity. Beyond ethical standards, integrity is *consistency* between our actions and our promises.

Fourth, virtues are universal, meaning that they are found in all great faiths, but they are not restricted to religions. There is plenty of evidence that across the major philosophical traditions around the world, character and virtues with different names and labels have been always considered for personal fulfillment and the flourishing of society. It means humanity has learned this upon the experience of thousands of years of civilization (Havard 2007).

Boston EI Questionnaire—An Exercise

In this exercise, you will be asked to do the Boston EI questionnaire[1] to evaluate your current level of emotional intelligence (EI). When completing the survey, you will see the improvement opportunities. These questions will help you assess how you perceive your emotional intelligence.

Remember that for us, emotional intelligence is the display on the surface of our level of character-building. Therefore, this exercise will expose signals of the existence or lack of character. We will offer, after this questionnaire, two more exercises that explore your character even deeper, giving you a more appropriate assessment on where you stand at the level of virtues.

At the end of the day, all these exercises will give you a complete test of your character fit for undertaking the development of the vision and goals that you have decided in the previous chapters. It is like when you want to start a sport and they need to check your physical fitness first!

For each question, you are asked to circle the closest possible answer to your feelings. As always, try to be honest; otherwise, there is no point in doing it!

Conclusions

Self-Awareness

What can I do to improve?

_____

_____

_____

_____

_____

_____

_____

_____

_____

---

[1]   Free of charge questionnaire available online. One of many sources: https://mtdsalestraining.com/wp-content/uploads/2013/01/Managing-Your-EQ-For-Better-Sales-Performance.pdf

Self-Regulation

What can I do to improve?

_____

_____

_____

_____

_____

_____

_____

_____

_____

Self-Motivation

What can I do to improve?

_____

_____

_____

_____

_____

_____

_____

_____

_____

Empathy

What can I do to improve?

_____

_____

_____

_____

_____

_____

_____

_____

_____

Social Skills

What can I do to improve?

Seligman Brief Strengths Test—An Exercise

As said before, we want to offer one more exercise on character, which is the real reason behind your EQ level. Seligman (one of the most renowned experts in positive psychology) with his Penn University team has developed one of the most ambitious projects in terms of character: Authentic Happiness.

Seligman offers many tests, but we suggest you do one: Brief Strengths Test. It focuses on your self-perceived best qualities. The test is found online under the following link:

https://authentichappiness.sas.upenn.edu/user/login?destination=node/504

We have already touched upon the importance of positive psychology and Seligman's ideas in the previous chapters—how you think about yourself has an impact on the way you contribute to yourself and other people.

Once you have completed the survey, you will be offered the results in comparison to other respondents. We encourage you to carefully read the results and write your own thoughts about them.

Conclusions from test

_____

_____

_____

_____

Now, please turn to the exercise in your personal and career journey "Leader's Journal" and start filling in your roadmap "Brief Strengths Test," as well as the conclusions from the tests.

Conclusions

In this chapter, we have in some way demystified the concept of emotional intelligence (EQ). On the one hand, we have highlighted its relevance, but on the other, the need to dig deeper on it understanding that EQ is not simply self-control, how to manage our emotions, but is rather what the Greeks called character-building.

In this chapter, we have also distinguished the differences between positive and negative habits and how to develop virtues that are the raw material of character. We understand that character is the real root of EQ and provides the personal strength in order to accomplish our previously decided goals daily.

We have also provided assessments and exercises that can help the reader to better understand these concepts. Character-building is in all regards the most important development path for any leader, as it is the only way to guarantee consistent growth and excellence in the long run.

CHAPTER 11

Growing Through Coaching and Sports Spirit

Introduction

The objective of this last chapter is to introduce a tool that can help you to grow in your personal leadership competences daily with the support of others. This tool, namely *coaching*, is a popular one, but it does not mean that it is neither the best one nor unique. Coaching has become very popular in the last few years partly because access to coaching training became more widespread across the world.

The reason we finish the workbook with coaching is because we want to highlight three of its characteristics that should be present in any assistance you might look for to move forward on your journey of growth:

- We always need a system of external support.
- We need to grow in self-confidence that is part of the methodology of coaching.
- We need to feel ownership over the process and results, which is also an essential element of coaching.

Coaching is generally associated with a profession of a coach; however, in the framework of this workbook, we look at coaching as a methodology of individual assistance that any manager or supervisor can exercise with their subordinates.

This chapter will start with the basic notions about coaching, then we will move into tips for being a good coach, and finally, we will offer an exercise in order to practice it.

Basic Ideas About Coaching

The *allegory of large spoons* (see figure 11.1) is a good representation of why coaching really is necessary in corporate settings: coaching allows people to share between each other their competencies and experiences. All of us have large spoons, meaning our knowledge, our background, and our expertise. These large spoons should be used in order not only to support other people, but also to support ourselves, creating more social cohesion in the teams. In some way, you want to create a more collective mindset around you, which is so important in a society where individualism is prevalent.

Figure 11.1 One human family, food for all

Source: (Caritas n.d.)

Coaching as a learning tool generally does not deal with technical skills that could be quickly learned. Coaching usually works in developing competencies that require long-term exercise. Coaching focuses on impacting the habits of the people, their character, what makes leaders consistent across circumstances, as we discussed in the previous chapter.

An essential idea about coaching, as a teaching or learning tool, is that the main activity of a coach is listening; meanwhile, other teaching methods imply instructions. An example in literature is Momo (Michael Ende).

> Momo listened to everyone and everything... even to the rain and the wind and the pine trees - and all of them spoke to her after their own fashion. Momo was staring at them wide-eyed,

but neither man quite knew how to interpret her gaze... Although her expression gave no clue, they suddenly seem to see themselves mirrored in her eyes and began to feel sheepish. She became so important to them that they wondered how they had ever managed without her in the past. And the longer she stayed with them, the more indispensable she became; so indispensable, in fact, that their one fear was that she might someday move on.

Momo was a coach not because she asked people to do things, but because she listened to them. That is how a modern leader must work. He or she must be able to listen to others, to help them break the wall of fear, and make the right decisions.

A good definition of coaching is the following:

Coaching is a relational process, based on a relationship of trust and commitment, conducted by two people (facilitator-guide coach and recipient-beneficiary-coachee) and undertaken in an organizational or work context, in which the coach uses conversation or dialogue to stimulate learning and induce the coachee to reflect on him/herself and his/her environment with the aim of defining goals, making decisions and acting to achieve them, for the coachee's own personal benefit and for the benefit of the organization (Larburu 2005).

It is important to highlight the key ideas of this definition:

1. *It is a relationship of trust*: There should be openness from both sides, what is not automatic, that requires time. There are two special ingredients for a coachee to trust the coach: the first one is the level of competence of the coach and the second one is the character of the coach. Topics that are dealt in coaching are so sensitive that any failure to generate trust can derail the whole process.
2. The second element is *that conversation and dialogue are there to stimulate learning*. In this sense, coaching is not initially intended as a replacement of psychologists, counselors, or friends.

3. Coaching has *one or more learning objectives* attached to each process. There are problems with which the coach should never deal with like psychological anomalies.

4. Coaching is generally done in an *organizational context* and should have a beneficial impact on the organization. Though many individuals look for coaching services on their own, a significant part of coaches work in cooperation with the specific organization. This means that the objective of the coaching process should be in alignment with the organizational objectives.

Managers as Coaches

Most of the leaders will not be in their life professional coaches, but as managers who want to become leaders, the coaching process will be very likely a part of their daily duties. A manager-coach can achieve three important objectives through coaching in their teams:

(1) They can help their subordinates to stay focused on the desired outcomes.
(2) They create a support system that encourages continuous development.
(3) They can help their subordinates to take small steps and keep on moving forward in their improvement.

A manager who uses coaching systematically is providing at the end of the day an inter-cooperative framework where subordinates through reflection can reach the maximum of their talents.

However, in order to exercise coaching, managers should develop the following competencies:

- Active listening
- Empathy
- Capacity for observation and diagnosis
- Ability to form relationships
- Ability to develop concepts and be creative
- Communication skills
- Flexibility

As we can see, it is not possible to improvise the character of a coach. The set of competencies that are needed require intensive training and practice. That is the reason for the proliferation of certification courses, though coaching could be trained in other settings as well.

GROW Model—An Exercise

We want you to have a test of how coaching works. Of course, this is not more than putting your fingers into the water. A coaching session can follow the GROW model, which is thought to help people to develop themselves. It is a very useful framework to structure a coaching process in general. You can find a suggested guide of the GROW model next.

We propose that you test it. In order to do that, you need to find two partners. You (A) will be the coach, one of your partners (B) will be the coaches, and the third one (C) will be controlling the time and observing the session. The first time, A coaches B. The second time, B coaches A. In both cases, the session should not last more than seven minutes.

Before you start, both (A) and (B) think on a particular life or career challenge they would like to discuss and get a coaching support: buying a new house, accepting a promotion, signing up for a master's program, and so on.

Before running the session, the three partners should study carefully the questions in order to make the most of the allocated time.

G Goal

Questions to consider

What do you want? or How will you know when you achieve it? When do you want to achieve it by? How achieving it will benefit you and the others?

_____

_____

_____

_____

_____

_____

_____

_____

R Reality

Questions to consider

What have you done specifically so far to achieve your goal? What challenges have you met and overcome? What other challenges do you expect to meet?

_____

_____

_____

_____

_____

_____

_____

_____

O Options

Questions to consider

What could you do? What else…? What if…?

_____

_____

_____

_____

_____

_____

_____

_____

W Will or Way Forward

Questions to consider

Which option would be fastest, easiest or preferred? What might stop you? When will you take action?

_____

_____

_____

_____

_____

_____

_____

_____

If you are using this workbook with the support of an instructor, you will not have difficulties understanding the task. It is even likely that you will be required to do it in class. If you do not have the support of an instructor, we suggest you look for additional material on the Internet and, if possible, a sample session on YouTube.

Coaching and Change

Essentially, coaching is a tool for learning, and learning is, as such, a process of change. Whenever we learn, there is some aspect of our intellectual, emotional, or physical sides that is changing. Change in learning implies that something we knew in one way before; we know it in a different way now. C. S. Lewis used to say that any learning process implies some sort of suffering. Therefore, this is the reason why the emotional support that a coach gives is so important.

The best way to describe in general terms the process of coaching is the change process designed by Schein. It has three steps: unfreezing the reality, accepting change, commitment and freezing the habit.

A. Unfreezing the reality: The first task of a coach is to help the coachee to accept his own reality and the reality of the outcome he wants to pursue.

B. Accepting change: The second task is to help the coachee to commit to the further development in the specific competence and to the very specific objectives in terms of growth.

C. Commitment and freezing the habit: The third task of the coach is to support the practice of the new habits that guarantees the long-term development of the desired competences.

The type of coaching that will be necessary depends on the difference between the personal perception of development and its external perception. If we get back to the process of change designed by Schein, the level of personal acceptance and commitment toward the development goals will be determinant for designing the coaching process that should be delivered.

For example, if there is an agreement between coach and coachee on the areas of improvement, the role of the coach will be more focused on the emotional support during the development of the new habits. This is what is called *supportive coaching* (see figure 11.2). If there is an agreement between a coach and coachee on the strengths, then again, the focus of the coaching process will be on the emotional support, but with a clear orientation toward reaching new heights, and therefore, it is called a *coaching of excellence*. Now, if the coach assesses as a strength what the

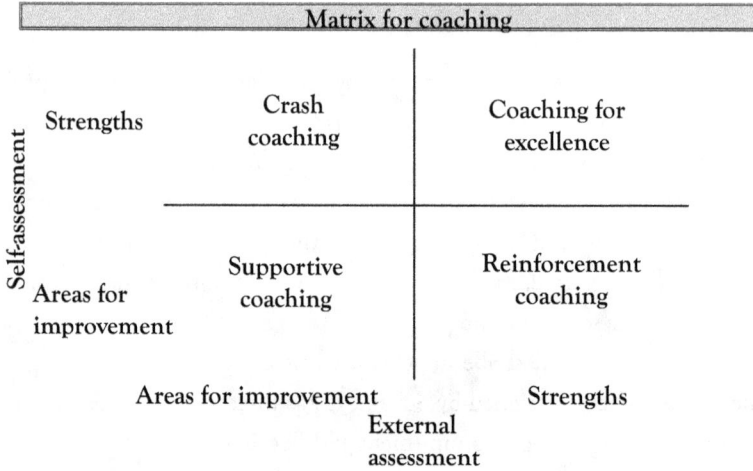

Figure 11.2 C matrix for coaching

Source: (García-Lombardía and Cardona 2005)

coachee sees as an area of improvement, the focus of the coaching will be strengthening the self-acceptance of the current virtues. In simple words, to improve the self-confidence of the coachee. This is called *reinforcement coaching*. However, if the coach recognizes as areas of improvement what the coachee perceives as strength, then the focus of the coachee will be increasing the reality check of the coachee. This is what is called *crash coaching* and generally is very necessary among successful executives.

How to Convince People on the Need of Coaching

As we have said, crash coaching used to be one of the most frequent among successful executives. One of the reasons, as Chris Argyris points out, is the substantial gap between *what people are* and *what they say they are*, especially among successful executives. We suggest simple questions that can be given to any manager to understand if they need support in their professional development. We encourage using these questions in a conversation about the need of coaching to break the ice, but certainly, they do not offer any complete assessment on the needs for coaching. The reason why they are effective is that these are very common behaviors among successful managers. Just ask the manager for yes or no to the following questions.

Are you…

- Lacking a mentor or a coach?
- Being overly demanding or ambitious?
- Failing to understand your subordinate?
- Do you have a tendency toward procrastination?
- Having difficulties to motivate people?
- Failing to build long-term relationships?
- Facing stress at the time of delivering complex projects?
- Are you suffering life–work imbalances?

If the answer to one or more of these items is yes, then you have a chance to start a meaningful conversation on the need for coaching. Of course, you must make these questions to yourself first!

Now, before we close, we want you to consider if you would not like to start trying coaching as a coach. We are not talking about professional coaching but as a manager-coach. Before you answer yes or no, consider what would it take for you to get the necessary competences.

Now, please turn to the exercise in your personal and career journey Leader's Journal and start filling in your roadmap 3.4. How will I improve my coaching and soft power skills during the next year (using GROW model)? When you have done the test, please fill out the conclusions from this test.

Conclusions

There are a variety of ways how to develop character and competencies; however, in this chapter, we have focused on coaching. Coaching could be a very powerful tool, as it provides the two main inputs for personal development, meaning emotional support and guidance. The wall of fear we mentioned in a previous chapter is always present, and we need someone who accompanies us in the process of crossing through it.

Though we provided a definition of coaching that is used in a variety of settings, we have focused in this chapter not so much in professional coaches but on managers that exercise coaching in their work with subordinates. In this way, these manager-coaches can create the corporate context where employees are encouraged to reflect on their careers and become less context-dependent, as we have seen in a previous chapter.

Developing coaching as a competence could be a very helpful mechanism to continuously developing all the concepts and ideas that have been exposed in this workbook on a daily basis. Even more, finding someone who supports us as a coach or in some coaching capacity will be determinant for the long-term success of the journey you have just started.

Brief Epilogue for a Long Book

The adventure of setting a workbook that can be used in different courses and trainings of self-leadership proved to be a very challenging task. Though we have been running personal development courses for many years, putting all our materials together in a way that can be useful for a wide range of instructors and students was not easy.

It took us roughly three years. Our busy lives and careers did not help to make the process smoother. Therefore, as we send the final book to the print, we feel very proud of our achievement. We have tested this book with many of our students and colleagues. We have received precious feedback, and we expect that as it starts to be used in different contexts, we will get even more comments that will help for the upgrades of the next editions.

As we were getting ready to finalize the manuscript, the COVID-19 pandemic impacted the world, the business world, and the education sector. As with any significant crisis, it has triggered a reflection process about our careers, lives, and principles. This crisis confirmed the need to have available materials and programs that provide frameworks to go through this reflection properly when the need appears. Crises and transitions are a normal pattern for managers; however, they are particularly challenging when they are acute and make an *unrequested visit* to our lives. Reflection allows people to put their thoughts together and understand the deepest motivations behind their efforts and decisions. We hope this book and its exercises will be suitable companions in this effort.

Dear reader: If you have gone already through this book, we congratulate you. It means you are very committed to your development. It means that you are taking ownership of your future. Is any other more critical attitude for success out there? Well done, keep going and help others on their own reflection process!

APPENDIX 1

The Syllabus of the Personal and Career Development Course on Which the Workbook is Based

Summer 2020

COURSE No.:	
PROGRAM:	Professional MBA
INSTRUCTOR:	Dr. Claudio Andres Rivera, Dr. Inese Muzikante (co-instructor)
CLASS DAYS AND TIME:	Tuesdays–Thursday 18.00–21.00
OFFICE LOCATION AND HOURS:	By appointment, Room 201
CONTACT PHONE:	
E-MAIL:	claudio.rivera@rbs.lv; inese.muzikante@gmail.com; elza.priede@rbs.lv

Literature

1 Suggested books

Just Enough: Tools for Creating Success in Your Work and Life. Laura Nash and Howard Stevenson

How to develop leadership competences. Pablo Cardona and Pilar Garcia-Lombardia

Growing as a leader. Pablo Cardona and Helen Wilkinson

Virtuous leadership. An agenda for personal excellence. Alexandre Havard

Masters of your destiny. Nuria Chinchilla

2 Cases, articles and other readings

A specific schedule of reading assignments is listed in the following calendar. You are responsible for having assigned texts read before class.

Course Objectives

Personal and Career Development strives to provide students with the capacity for taking small and big decisions with regard of their career and personal development plans. In this course, students learn how to "build and implement their career plan" based on their lives' bigger picture.

Upon completion of this course, you should be able:

- To assess your strengths, interests, and priorities for your career and life
- To develop a personal and career development plan
- To identify career opportunities, which are aligned with your other personal objectives
- To develop an action plan for improving your skills and addressing conflicting goals
- To improve your capacity for coaching others
- To understand the power of interpersonal relationships and how to keep them in the long run

Course Overview

All of us want to do something remarkable with our lives and our careers. With this course, we want to help you learn how to select your goals and how to use your energy and skills to accomplish them. This course aims to assist you in understanding what success really means for you and how to get there.

We will start the journey by helping you to improve your self-knowledge, discover your values, and build your personal vision. In a second step, we will help you to align your career plan with your other goals in life, your competences, and your context. The program will move forward then to a third part, where we will help you understand how to implement your career and life plans in your daily life. Finally, you will work on your relationships, understanding how to build lasting partnerships within your family, your acquaintances, colleagues, and friends.

Personal and Career Development takes a very practical approach. During the course, we will use state-of-the-art tools and knowledge. Faculty will use evaluation and self-awareness tools and a broad range of activities to identify, enhance, and challenge your capabilities and ideas: simulations, case studies, tests, indoor exercises, group discussions, workshops, coaching, and a bit—only a little bit—of lecturing and reading! In addition, you will maintain a learning log throughout the program to facilitate your reflection.

Electronic Resources

The databases maintained by the RBS library are a valuable student resource. Therefore, it is required that you use this resource during your coursework. There are a selection of readings in the schedule that are found through the databases. In addition, it is expected that you will access current research materials in the databases for your individual assignment. Your ability to correctly use a wide range of literature from the databases will influence your grade on your individual assignment.

Course Requirements and Assignments

There are six assignments that compose your grade: two case write-ups (your choice of cases), one learning log (your choice), Reflected Best Self paper, class participation, a group paper and presentation, and a final paper[1]. I describe briefly the assignments, though we are going to talk in detail about each one during the first class.

(1) *Two Case Write-ups (10% total, 5% for each case write-up)*—electronic submission
    You are required to submit two case write-ups. You may choose from any of the four cases listed in class schedule. The write-ups should be

---

[1] Assignments *Learning log* and *Reflected Best Self* are modifications of similar assignments used in the course *Principled Leadership* at Goizueta Business School.

typed, no more than two pages in length (12 pt. font, single spaced) and consist of your answers to the Discussion Questions posted in ORTUS. The write-ups are meant to help you develop your analytical skills and prepare you for participating in class. *Your case write-up is due in class on the day that the case is assigned; no late write-ups will be accepted.*

(2) *One Learning Log—Choose one option (15%):* electronic submission
The learning log provides you with an opportunity to reflect on the ways in which the issues and concepts raised in class affect you personally and your life career decisions. The questions to be answered in these logs appear as follows. You have the option to select one of these logs and complete it on time. Your learning log should be no more than three pages (double-spaced). I will evaluate the logs based upon how reflective, attractive, practical, and well organized they are.

Learning Log A: To Trust or Not to Trust

Purpose: Trust and integrity are perhaps the most critical values and principles that leaders have. In this learning log, you analyze how you lead through trusting or distrusting others.

1. Think of two people whom you know fairly well: one whom you trust and one whom you do not trust.
2. List the reasons that lead you to trust or distrust each person (no need to identify the real person—use disguised names and identifying information).
3. What do you do to communicate to each person that you trust or do not trust them (i.e., what are the behaviors that you are doing that engender trust or distrust)?
4. What, if anything, could the person you distrust do to earn your trust?
5. Assume you decide to give to the person you distrust a new chance. What words, images, phrases, and metaphors would you see as most critical for conveying or creating a set of principles for your relationship? Justify your choices.
6. What do you have to do to enable this to happen? What do you do to win the trust of others?

Learning Log B: Am I Ready to Take the Risk?

Purpose: People, who have been successful in life and career in the long run, share at least one common characteristic: they really love what they have been doing during most of their lives. However, to do what we love implies often to take certain risks.

1. Pick and describe a project (business, social, personal, etc.) you madly desire to undertake.
2. Explain how the process of implementing this project could impact positively or negatively the four categories of success: happiness, achievement, legacy, and significance.
3. Based upon the project you have identified, which are the 2–3 competencies you realistically think you need to focus on and develop? Please give reasons.
4. Assume you decide to take the risks and undertake the project. What words, images, phrases, and metaphors would you see as most critical for conveying or explaining your motivation and decision? Justify your choices.

(3) *Best-Self Portrait (10%)—DUE class no. 5*: electronic submission
This exercise provides you with feedback about who you are when you are at your best. You will request positive feedback from significant people in your lives, which you will then synthesize into a cumulative portrait of your *best-self*. The exercise can be used as a tool for personal development because it enables you to identify your unique strengths and talents. The process of getting feedback will begin immediately and your Best-Self Portrait is due in class 5. Your portrait should be approximately 2–4 pages in length (double-spaced, 12 pt. font, 1" margins) and should focus on your interpretation of the feedback you receive. More details will be given in class. However, I strongly recommend that you start as soon as possible. Your Best-Self Portrait will not be evaluated on the basis of who you are, but rather on the quality of your reflection and the ability to express it.

(4) *Class Participation (15—*Self-assessment and minimum

Because of the nature of the course, attendance and participation are critical and an essential part of your grade. You are expected to attend each class having read all assigned readings and having prepared assignments, case questions, or other discussion points. If a reading assignment is listed as a case, you should be prepared to discuss the case and answer all the assigned questions provided in the course's materials.

In this course, our goal is to create an environment where you and your classmates could feel confident in participating, discussing, arguing, and sharing. Any behaviors that could harm the learning environment will be evaluated negatively. I commit to be courteous, kind, professional, and have an opinion and respect others' rights to hold opinions and beliefs that differ from my own. I expect that you will too!

Your class participation grade *will be self-assessed.* In any case, lack of attendance to the course will imply a reduction of 10 points per absence and 40 percent of the total grade of the course if you do not attend more than seven lectures. Every class will start with a 10-minute team discussion.

(5) *Group Project*: Presentation and Paper (25%). Group paper due class no. 14. Electronic submission

Presentations will be scheduled on the last days of the class (see syllabus). Your paper is due the last day of class.

In other course assignments, such as the learning logs and the Best-Self Portrait, you will (hopefully) come to understand yourself better, in terms of your values, personality, and behaviors. The objectives of the group project are different:

1. That you could check out your understanding of the main issues of this course with your peers
2. That you could observe the connection between personal development and innovation or crisis

More details will follow in class. Briefly, though, you will work in small groups (of about 5 students/project). You could choose either of the following options. You are required to present your findings in class and submit a paper (approximately 10–15 pp in length). Each student will be asked to complete a peer evaluation.

Option A: *Study of managers' innovation skills*
You conduct a study of managers (under condition of anonymity), identifying 3–7 (at international, national, or local level), interviewing them personally and supplementing the interviews with any secondary information. Following a similar protocol of a study published at Harvard Business Review, your study will have three parts:

(a) A questionnaire on managers' innovation skills
(b) A questionnaire on character strengths (I will provide it)
(c) Other questions your team would like to add

You will be able to run the study among other classmates, if they do not belong to your team.

Option B: Personal development under crisis
Crisis is one of the most relevant grounds for personal development. We will work intensively on this during the course. In the last few years, we have seen no shortage of crises of any sort. Currently, for example, the impact of COVID-19 crisis will be a ground of success and failures for many public and business leaders.

To prompt your ideas, here are some possibilities that could lead to projects (although you are not limited to these):

- COVID-19
- Reform of Latvian financial sector
- Latvijas Bankas crisis
- Latvian education system reform
- Zolitūdes crisis
- Crisis in Ukraine
- War in Afghanistan
- Hurricane Katrina
- 9/11 aftermath

- Political crisis in Latvia in 2019
- Revolution in Egypt
- The financial crisis in Latvia
- Wikileaks
- Norway's massacre of 2011
- Bankruptcy of Lehman Brothers

As a group, you will need to choose a recent, visible, public crisis and focus on *one key aspect (portion) of that crisis.* Locate publicly available information on this aspect of the crisis, through the Internet, newspapers, magazines, books, and so on (and, if possible, contacting any of those involved in the crisis). Focus on understanding how value- and vision-based leadership is effective, ineffective, and/or absent in the situation. Examine:

- What vision and values are evident in the crisis? What values are missing?
- Where does vision and value-based leadership occur? And, where is it missing? Be sure to examine:
  ○ Individual leaders, both formally appointed and informally emergent
  ○ Organizational, governmental (local, national), societal, cultural, and other systems that may function to support (or not support) vision and value-based leadership and action
- Why is this so? Why does vision and value-based leadership emerge where it does…and why is it absent when perhaps it should be working?
- From your analysis, please answer to this question: how can you use your values and vision to be helpful in a time of crisis?

(6) *Exam—Personal and Career Roadmap*: 25% of grade. Hard-copy submission
You are going to submit your final paper on the last day of the course. The paper is set up in a way that will help you to review all the topics we will discuss in class and your own personal learning. More details will follow.

Make-up exams: Make-up exams for the mid-term and the final are generally not given. If there are extenuating circumstances and you must miss an exam, the instructor must be notified ahead of time. The only time a make-up exam can be taken is during the week following the date of the exam. If a student does not notify the instructor of an absence or misses the make-up exam deadline, the exam will not be included in the final grade.

Grading

Grading for the course is as follows:

Assignments	Points
Case memos 2@50 pts each	100
Learning log	150
Best-Self Portrait	100
Group Project	250
Exam—Personal and Career Roadmap	250
Class participation—Self-Evaluation Form	150
TOTAL	1,000

Final grades are calculated on the following basis.

> 949	=	10
850–949	=	9
750–849	=	8
650–749	=	7
550–649	=	6
450–549	=	5
350–449	=	4
< 350	=	failing

Your grades will be updated regularly on the online assistant. Please check to see that your grades are recorded correctly.

Academic Integrity

In an effort to strengthen ethics within Riga Business School (RBS) and the business community, the RBS policy is to take steps to avoid cases of academic fraud. To achieve this, several websites are available to help familiarize you with issues of cheating and plagiarism and how to avoid them. Please review these sights and learn how to correctly reference all of your work. "I didn't know" will not be an acceptable excuse.

Be aware that any student who turns in written work that is not original with incorrectly referenced sources (i.e., plagiarized) will be subject to the RBS sanctions policy on Academic Fraud (see the policy on the online assistant). Of course, the same consequences apply to academic dishonesty on tests and quizzes.

To find information on what plagiarism is and how to avoid it, please visit the links at:

http://uottawa.ca/plagiarism.pdf

http:// socialsciences.uottawa.ca/pdf/plagiarism2.pdf

http://sass.uottawa.ca/writing/plagiarism.pdf

This short presentation on research and plagiarism will also help learn to correctly reference sources and provide good advice on research:

http://library.acadiau.ca/tutorials/plagiarism/

Class Schedule

A specific schedule of readings and assignments is listed next. You are responsible for having assigned readings and assignments read before class. Schedule is provisional; changes will be announced in advance. A number of readings will be handed over to you before the beginning of the course. They will be ordered according to the class where is going to be used.

Class	Topic	Pre- readings and submissions
Part 1: Taking ownership of your life		
Class 1 05–05	18.00–20.00 *Claudio Rivera* • Course opening. Me, Inc. Self-leadership and purpose • Test #1 on Development Needs • Syllabus intro 20.00–21.00 *Inese Muzikante* • Presentation of the Peer Evaluation Form and Team presentations • Best-Self Portrait	• Suggested reading: book *Just Enough* by Laura Nash and Howard Stevenson. Part One. • *"Self-management: self-knowledge, self-control and self-esteem"*, Alberto Ribera

Class	Topic	Pre- readings and submissions
Class 2 07–05	*18.00–20.00 Claudio Rivera* • Self-awareness: under-standing the inner self • Personality Test #2 *20.00–21.00 Inese Muzikante* • Presentation of the Personal and Career Roadmap	• <u>**Case study**</u> Fernando Ruiz (**A, B, and D**) • Article *"Motivation, Leadership, and Organization: Do American Theories Apply Abroad"* by Geert Hofstede • Paper *"Cultural values in organizations: insights for Europe"* L. Sagiv and S. Schwartz.
Class 3 12–05	*18.00–20.00 Claudio Rivera* • Core Personal Values—The seven levels of values • Test #3 on Cultural Dif-ferences • Test #4 on Personal Values *20.00–21.00 Guest Speaker*	• <u>**Case study**</u> **La Fageda: an outrageous initiative** • *Selected papers* of Richard Barret • *Beyond Selfishness* by Mintzberg and others • Article *The Moral Dilemmas of Modern Society* by Charles Handy • *Suggested reading:* book *"Building a Values-Driven Organization: A Whole System Approach to Cultural Transfor-mation"* by Richard Barrett. Chapters 2 and 5.
Class 4 14–05	Indoor/Outdoor Activity	
Class 5 19–05	*18.00–20.00 Claudio Rivera* • Building a personal vision and strategy • Vision building exercise • Wrap-up of Part 1 *20.00–21.00 Guest Speaker*	• <u>**Best-Self Portrait due**</u> • Steve Jobs' Stanford Commencement Speech (2005)—Available on YouTube • Movie: Last lecture of Randy Pausch. We will screen it on a specific day but you could watch it in your own. • Suggested reading: *Vision Com-petency: the direction of the leader,* excerpt from book *Leadership: from Mystery to Mastery* by Larry Stout • Suggested reading: book *"Man's Search for Meaning"* by Viktor Frankl
	Part 2: Taking ownership of your career	
Class 6 21–05	*18.00–20.00 Claudio Rivera* • Managing the career by personal vision. • The Kaleidoscope strategy *20.00–21.00 Inese Muzikante* • Debriefing Best-Self Portrait • Learning Log – Q&A	• <u>**Personal and Career Development Roadmap part 1 due**</u> • Movie: "Citizen Kane" • Technical note on the Kaleidoscope strategy by C. Rivera • Suggested reading: book *Just Enough* by Laura Nash and Howard Steven-son. Part Two.

Class	Topic	Pre- readings and submissions
Class 7 26–05	*18.00–20.00 Claudio Rivera* • Assessment of context and competencies *20.00–21.00 Inese Muzikante* • General feedback of Roadmaps • Personal and Career Development Roadmap 2nd part - Q&A	• VIA signature strengths questionnaire (instructions in class) • Excerpt from book "The Innovator's DNA: Mastering the Five Skills of Disruptive Innovators" by Jeff Dyer and others
Class 8 28–05	Career development plan	• <u>Learning Log due</u> • <u>Case study</u> Rob Parson at Morgan Stanley (A)
Class 9 02–06	*18.00–20.00 Claudio Rivera* • Competences Development plan • Risk, recovery, and resilience • Wrap-up of Part 2 *20.00–21.00 Guest Speaker*	• Materials uploaded in ORTUS
Part 3: Taking ownership of your daily agenda		
Class 10 04–06	*18.00–20.00 Claudio Rivera* • GROW Model • Life Balance and Time Management *20.00–21.00 Inese Muzikante* • Last assignments – Q&A	• <u>**Personal and Career Development Roadmap part 2 due**</u> • Selected materials on Virtuous Leadership • Character strengths and virtues (technical note) by Alberto Ribera • Suggested reading: book *Just Enough* by Laura Nash and Howard Stevenson. Part Three and book *Virtuous Leadership* by Alexandre Havard
Class 11 09–06	• Growing through coaching and sports spirit • General feedback of Roadmaps • Wrap-up of Part 3	• Team experience with coaching

Class	Topic	Pre- readings and submissions
Part 4: Taking ownership of your relationships		

Class 12
11-06
	• The art of friendship and partnership
	• Personal development network exercise
		• <u>Personal and Career Development Roadmap part 3 due</u>
		• <u>Case study</u> Victorinox: 125 Years in the Cutting Edge
		  • *Persuasion: a* rhetorical approach (technical note) by Prof. Brian O.C. Legget
		  • Article Managing Multicultural Teams by Brett and others

Class 13 16-06	• 1st session of group presentations	
Class 14 18-06	• 2nd session of group presentations • Informal closing of course	• **Group Paper due** • **Personal and Career Development Roadmap due**

APPENDIX 2

My Personal and Career Journey "Leader's Journal"

RBS

RIGA BUSINESS SCHOOL

Riga Technical University

Personal and Career Development

Final Assignment

My Personal and Career Journey Leader's Journal

Table of Contents

1. Owning My Life

1.1. Self-Awareness

1.1.1. My Personality According to Keirsey Test

1. Which is my personality?

2. What developmental potential still exists for me based on my current traits?

3. What potential derailment risks do I have because of my personality?

1.1.2. The Best-Self Portrait and/or VIA Test

Conclusions From These Tests

1. What strengths have I developed at my current life stage?

2. What developmental potential still exists for me based on tests' results?

3. What potential derailment risks do I have based on this tests' results?

1.1.3. The Impact of My Culture (Hofstede Test)

Conclusions From This Test

1. What strengths have I developed because of the impact of my culture?

2. What developmental potential still exists for me because of the impact of my culture?

3. What potential derailment risks do I have because of the impact of my culture?

1.1.4. My Value Scale (Barret Test)

Conclusions From This Test

1. Which are my predominant values and my current level of motivation (1–7)?

2. What developmental potential still exists for me because my current value scale?

3. What potential derailment risks do I have because of my current value scale?

1.2. *My Kaleidoscope (Kaleidoscope Strategy)*

Insert your current Kaleidoscope.

Conclusions From the Kaleidoscope

1. Are some chambers empty?

2. Are others too full?

3. Where am I devoting most of my strengths and time?

4. Indicate how my personality, values, culture, and strengths set have impacted in my current Kaleidoscope.

Insert my desirable Kaleidoscope in 2030.

1.3. My Vision in 2030 Based on the Kaleidoscope

1.4. My "Energizing" Mission to Move Forward

(a person, a cause, a specific painful situation, ...)

2. Owning My Career

2.1. Retro Analysis (Based on IESE Test)

Insert the corresponding graphs.

2.2. My Current Career

2.2.1 General Questions About Your Current Position

(includes your MBA studies)

(a) What is my view of current situation?

(b) What strengths come to me naturally in my current position?

(c) What do I do well?

(d) What appeals to me in my current position?

(e) A SWOT analysis of my current employment situation.

2.2.2. Assessment of My Short-Term Competencies Development Needs (Includes Your MBA Studies)

(a) My most important goal/challenge in the short term in my current position or career (one-two years' time span).

(b) List of the top 5–10 contributions needed from me in order to successfully achieve this goal/challenge.

(c) List of the needed competences in order to implement these contributions.

2.2.3. Action Contract

(a) The one or two competences (out of the list in 2.2.2.c) I need to develop further in order to accomplish the goal/challenge and future similar goals/challenges.

(b) The 2–3 SMART[1] objectives for each of the competencies/skills I think I should develop.

(c) Which is the method that can help me most in my action plan implementation?

2.3. My Second Curve

2.3.1. My Career Goal for 2022

2.3.2. My 2030 Vision

2.3.3. The Ideal Job Situation, Which Could Make This Vision Come True

2.3.4. My Personal SWOT Analysis Based on All the Previous Sections of This Paper

---

[1] Specific—Objectives should specify what they want to achieve.

[2] Measurable—You should be able to measure whether you are meeting the objectives or not.

[3] Achievable—Are the objectives you set achievable and attainable?

[4] Realistic—Can you realistically achieve the objectives with the resources you have?

[5] Time—When do you want to achieve the set objectives?

2.3.5. Action Contract

(d) The 1–2 main goals I need to accomplish in order to achieve the ideal job situation.

(e) The 2–3 SMART objectives for each of the competencies/skills I think I should develop. (Please take into account you are part of a MBA program.)

2.4. Dealing With My Derailment Risks During My Transitions

Derailment	How does or could it cause my derailment?	How will I overcome this potential derailment risk?
Keep doing what is made me successful until now		
Assume that others are motivated by the same things I am		
Do not send clear messages—about my values and my expectations		
Avoid unpleasant relationships		
Concentrate on the task, not relationship		
Let my failures define me		

3. Owning My Daily Agenda

3.1. The Dimension/s of EQ Where I Need Further Improvement (Based on the results of the Boston EI Questionnaire) are

3.2. The 2–3 Habits I Would Like to Pay Attention During the Next Year (Based on the "Guiding Questionnaire for Personal Reflection" provided in Appendix 7)

3.3. My "Standard Weekly Agenda" for the Next 365 Days (Excluding Holidays) Taking Carefully into Account My Desirable Kaleidoscope and Sections 2.3.4/2.2.3

4. Owning My Relationships

4.1. The Current Map of My Network Here (DNQ Exercise[2])

4.2. Conclusions Based on My Network:

1. What is missing?

2. Is it skewed toward career or psychological assistance?

3. Does the perfect mentor exist?

4. What is the relevance of my network in my personal development?

4.3. How I Will Improve My Coaching and Soft Power Skills During the Next Year (Using the GROW Model)

4.4. Based on Victorinox and La Fageda Cases[3], I Indicate How I can Transform My Team or Unit or Company in a Mission-Based Team or Unit or Company (Using the GROW Model)

---

[2] DNQ Exercise is available at Harvard Business School Publishing. It may be purchased through HBSP (paper questionnaire is #404-105 and CD instrument is #405-701) and there is a teaching note as well (#405-039).

[3] Both cases may be purchased through IESE Publishing. Victorinox: Victorinox: 125 Years in the Cutting Edge, #DPO-202-E. La Fageda: La Fageda 1982-2008: An Outrageous Initiative, #Case M-1218-E

5. Epilogue: I am Who I Wanted to Become (Letter Written to ... in August 2030)

6. Appendices

6.1 My Best-Self Portrait (See instructions in the Personal and Career Development Course Syllabus, Appendix 1)

6.2 What I Learned on My Way (The Learning Log) (See instructions in the Personal and Career Development Course Syllabus, Appendix 1)

6.3 You Can Add More if You Want

APPENDIX 3

The Keirsey Temperament Sorter

For each question, decide on answer **a** or **b** and put a check mark in the proper column of the answer sheet.

1. When the phone rings, do you
    a. Hurry to get to it first?
    b. Hope someone will answer?
2. Are you more
    a. Observant than introspective?
    b. Introspective than observant?
3. Is it worse to
    a. Have your head in the clouds?
    b. Be in a rut?
4. With people, are you usually more
    a. Firm than gentle?
    b. Gentle than firm?
5. Are you more comfortable in making
    a. Critical judgments?
    b. Value judgments?
6. Is clutter in the workplace something you
    a. Take time to straighten up?
    b. Tolerate pretty well?
7. Is it your way to
    a. Make up your mind quickly?
    b. Pick and choose at some length?
8. Waiting in line, do you often
    a. Chat with others?
    b. Stick to business?

9. Are you more
    a.Sensible than ideational?
    b.Ideational than sensible?
10. Are you more interested in
    a. What is actual?
    b. What is possible?
11. In making up your mind, are you more likely
    a. To go by data?
    b. To go by desires?
12. In sizing up others, do you tend to be
    a. Objective and impersonal?
    b. Friendly and personal?
13. Do you prefer contracts to be
    a. Signed, sealed, and delivered?
    b. Settled on a handshake?
14. Are you more satisfied having
    a. A finished product?
    b. Work in progress?
15. At a party, do you
    a. Interact with many, even strangers?
    b. Interact with a few friends?
16. Do you tend to be more
    a. Factual than speculative?
    b. Speculative than factual?
17. Do you like writers who
    a. Say what they mean?
    b. Use metaphors and symbolism?
18. Which appeals to you more
    a. Consistency of thought?
    b. Harmonious relationships?
19. If you must disappoint someone, are you
    a. Usually frank and straightforward?
    b. Warm and considerate?
20. On the job, do you want your activities
    a. Scheduled?
    b. Unscheduled?

21. Do you more often prefer
    a..Final, unalterable statements?
    b. Tentative, preliminary statements?
22. Does interacting with strangers
    a. Energize you?
    b. Tax your reserves?
23. Facts
    a. Speak for themselves
    b. Illustrate principles
24. Do you find visionaries and theorists
    a. Somewhat annoying?
    b. Rather fascinating?
25. In a heated discussion, do you
    a. Stick to your guns?
    b. Look for common ground?
26. Is it better to be
    a. Just?
    b. Merciful?
27. At work, is it more natural for you to
    a. Point out mistakes?
    b. Try to please others?
28. Are you more comfortable
    a. After a decision?
    b. Before a decision?
29. Do you tend to
    a. Say right out what is on your mind?
    b. Keep your ears open?
30. Common sense is
    a. Usually reliable
    b. Frequently questionable
31. Children often do not
    a. Make themselves useful enough
    b. Exercise their fantasy enough
32. When in charge of others, do you tend to be
    a. Firm and unbending?
    b. Forgiving and lenient?

33. Are you more often
    a. A cool-headed person?
    b. A warm-hearted person?
34. Are you prone to
    a. Nailing things down?
    b. Exploring the possibilities?
35. In most situations, are you more
    a. Deliberate than spontaneous?
    b. Spontaneous than deliberate?
36. Do you think of yourself as
    a. An outgoing person?
    b. A private person?
37. Are you more frequently
    a. A practical sort of person?
    b. A fanciful sort of person?
38. Do you speak more in
    a. Particulars than generalities?
    b. Generalities than particular?
39. Which is more of a compliment:
    a. "There's a logical person"
    b. "There's a sentimental person"
40. Which rules you more?
    a. Your thoughts
    b. Your feelings
41. When finishing a job, do you like to
    a. Tie up all the loose ends?
    b. Move on to something else?
42. Do you prefer to work
    a. To deadlines?
    b. Just whenever?
43. Are you the kind of person who
    a. Is rather talkative?
    b. Does not miss much?
44. Are you inclined to take what is said
    a. More literally?
    b. More figuratively?

45. Do you more often see
    a. What is right in front of you?
    b. What can only be imagined?
46. Is it worse to be
    a. Softy?
    b. Hard-nosed?
47. In trying circumstances, are you sometimes
    a. Too unsympathetic?
    b. Too sympathetic?
48. Do you tend to choose
    a. Rather carefully?
    b. Somewhat impulsively?
49. Are you inclined to be more
    a. Hurried than leisurely?
    b. Leisurely than hurried?
50. At work, do you tend to
    a. Be sociable with your colleagues?
    b. Keep more to yourself?
51. Are you more likely to trust
    a. Your experiences?
    b. Your conceptions?
52. Are you more inclined to feel
    a. Down to earth?
    b. Somewhat removed?
53. Do you think of yourself as a
    Tough-minded person?
    Tender-hearted person?
54. Do you value in yourself more that you are
    a. Reasonable?
    b. Devoted?
55. Do you usually want things
    a. Settled and decided?
    b. Just penciled in?
56. Would you say, you are more
    a. Serious and determined
    b. Easy going

57. Do you consider yourself
    a. A good conversationalist?
    b. A good listener?
58. Do you prize in yourself
    a. A strong hold on reality?
    b. A vivid imagination?
59. Are you drawn more to
    a. Fundamentals?
    b. Overtones?
60. Which seems the greater fault
    a. To be too compassionate?
    b. To be too dispassionate?
61. Are you swayed more by
    a. Convincing evidence?
    b. A touching appeal?
62. Do you feel better about
    a. Coming to closure?
    b. Keeping your options open?
63. Is it preferable mostly to
    a. Make sure things are arranged?
    b. Just let things happen naturally?
64. Are you inclined to be
    a. Easy to approach?
    b. Somewhat reserved?
65. In stories, do you prefer
    a. Action and adventure?
    b. Fantasy and heroism?
66. Is it easier for you to
    a. Put others to good use?
    b. Identify with others?
67. Which do you wish more for yourself?
    a. Strength of will
    b. Strength of emotion
68. Do you see yourself as basically
    a. Thick-skinned?
    b. Thin-skinned?

69. Do you tend to notice
    a. Disorderliness?
    b. Opportunities for change?
70. Are you more
    a. Routinized than whimsical?
    b. Whimsical than routinized?

Answer Sheet

Enter a check for each answer in the column for a or b.

	a	b		a	b		a	b		a	b		a	b		a	b		a	b		a	b
1			2			3			4			5			6			7		
8			9			10			11			12			13			14		
15			16			17			18			19			20			21		
22			23			24			25			26			27			28		
29			30			31			32			33			34			35		
36			37			38			39			40			41			42		
43			44			45			46			47			48			49		
50			51			52			53			54			55			56		
57			58			59			60			61			62			63		
64			65			66			67			68			69			70		

1   2   3   4   3   4   5   6   5   6   7   8   7   8

1   2   3   4   .   5   6   7   8

E I   S N   T F   J P

Directions for Scoring

1. **Add down** so that the total number of a answers is written in the box at the bottom of each column. Do the same for the b answers you have checked. Each of the 14 boxes should have a number it.

2. **Transfer the number** in box #1 of the answer grid to box #1 below the answer grid. Do this for box # 2 as well. Note, however, that you have two numbers for boxes 3 through 8. Bring down the first number for each box beneath the second, as indicated by the arrows. Now add all the pairs of numbers and enter the total in the boxes below the answer grid, so each box has only one number.

3. **Now you have** four pairs of numbers. Circle the letter below the larger numbers of each pair. If the two numbers of any pair are equal, then circle neither, but put a large X below them and circle it.

You have not identified your type. It should be one of the following:

Four SP [Artisans]
ESTP [Promoter]
ISTP [Crafter]
ESFP [Performer]
ISFP [Composer]

Four SF [Guardians]
ESTJ [Supervisor]
ISTJ [Inspector]
ESFJ [Provider]
ISFJ [Protector]

Four NF [Idealists]
ENFJ [Teacher]
INFJ [Counselor]
ENFP [Champion]
INFP [Healer]

Four NT [Rationals]
ENTJ [Field marshal]
INTJ [Mastermind]
ENTP [Inventor]
INTP [Architect]

You have not identified your type. It should be one of the following:

Four SP [Artisans]
ESTP [Promoter]
ISTP [Crafter]
ESFP [Performer]
ISFP [Composer]

Four SF [Guardians]
ESTJ [Supervisor]
ISTJ [Inspector]
ESFJ [Provider]
ISFJ [Protector]

Four NF [Idealists]
ENFJ [Teacher]
INFJ [Counselor]
ENFP [Champion]
INFP [Healer]

Four NT [Rationals]
ENTJ [Field marshal]
INTJ [Mastermind]
ENTP [Inventor]
INTP [Architect]

APPENDIX 4

Geert Hofstede's Work on Cultural Differences

Cultural Dimensions

Geert Hofstede analyzed a large database of employee values scores collected by IBM between 1967 and 1973 covering more than 70 countries, from which he first used the 40 largest only and afterwards extended the analysis to 50 countries and 3 regions. In the editions of GH's work since 2001, scores are listed for 74 countries and regions, partly based on replications and extensions of the IBM study on different international populations.

Subsequent studies validating the earlier results have included commercial airline pilots and students in 23 countries, civil service managers in 14 counties, 'up-market' consumers in 15 countries and 'elites' in 19 countries.

From the initial results, and later additions, Hofstede developed a model that identifies four primary Dimensions to assist in differentiating cultures: Power Distance - PDI, Individualism - IDV, Masculinity - MAS, and Uncertainty Avoidance - UAI.

Geert Hofstede added a fifth Dimension after conducting an additional international study with a survey instrument developed with Chinese employees and managers.

That Dimension, based on Confucian dynamism, is Long-Term Orientation - LTO and was applied to 23 countries. These five Hofstede Dimensions can also be found to correlate with other country, cultural, and religious paradigms.

The five cultural dimensions

Power Distance Index (PDI):

That is the extent to which the less powerful members of organizations and institutions (like the family) accept and expect that power is distributed unequally. This represents inequality (more versus less), but defined from below, not from above. It suggests that a society's level of inequality is endorsed by the followers as much as by the leaders. Power and inequality, of course, are extremely fundamental facts of any society and anybody with some international experience will be aware that 'all societies are unequal, but some are more unequal than others'.

Individualism (IDV):

On the one side versus its opposite, collectivism, that is the degree to which individuals are inte-grated into groups. On the individualist side we find societies in which the ties between individuals are loose: everyone is expected to look after him/herself and his/her immediate family. On the collectivist side, we find societies in which people from birth onwards are integrated into strong, cohesive in-groups, often extended families (with uncles, aunts and grandparents) which continue protecting them in exchange for unquestioning loyalty. The word 'collectivism' in this sense has no political meaning: it refers to the group, not to the state. Again, the issue addressed by this dimension is an extremely fundamental one, regarding all societies in the world.

Masculinity (MAS)

Versus its opposite, femininity refers to the distribution of roles between the genders which is another fundamental issue for any society to which a range of solutions are found. The IBM studies revealed that (a) women's values differ less among societies than men's values; (b) men's values from one country to another contain a dimension from very assertive and competitive and maximally different from women's values on the one side, to modest and caring and similar to women's values on the other. The assertive pole has been called 'masculine' and the modest, caring pole 'feminine'. The women in feminine countries have the same modest, caring values as the men; in the masculine countries they are somewhat assertive and competitive, but not as much as the men, so that these countries show a gap between men's values and women's values.

Uncertainty Avoidance Index (UAI)

Deals with a society's tolerance for uncertainty and ambiguity; it ultimately refers to man's search for Truth. It indicates to what extent a culture programs its members to feel either uncomfortable or comfortable in unstructured situations. Unstructured situations are novel, unknown, surprising and different from usual. Uncertainty avoidance cultures try to minimize the possibility of such situations by strict laws and rules, safety and security measures, and on the philosophical and religious level by a belief in absolute Truth; "there can only be one Truth and we have it".

People in uncertainty avoidance countries are also more emotional, and motivated by inner nervous energy. The opposite type, uncertainty accepting cultures, are more tolerant of opinions different from what they are used to; they try to have as few rules as possible, and on the philosophical and religious level they are relativist and allow many currents to flow side by side. People within these cultures are more phlegmatic and contemplative, and not expected by their environment to express emotions.

Long-Term Orientation (LTO)

Versus short-term orientation: this fifth dimension was found in a study among students in 23 countries around the world, using a questionnaire designed by Chinese scholars It can be said to deal with Virtue regardless of Truth. Values associated with Long Term Orientation are thrift and perseverance; values associated with Short Term Orientation are respect for tradition, fulfilling social obligations, and protecting one's 'face'. Both the positively and the negatively rated values of this dimension are found in the teachings of Confucius, the most influential Chinese philosopher who lived around 500 B.C.; however, the dimension also applies to countries without a Confucian heritage.

PDI	Power Distance Index	
IDV	Individualism	
MAS	Masculinity	
UAI	Uncertainty Avoidance Index	
LTO	Long-Term Orientation	

Country	PDI	IDV	MAS	UAI	LTO
Arab World **	80	38	52	68	
Argentina	49	46	56	86	
Australia	36	90	61	51	31
Austria	11	55	79	70	
Belgium	65	75	54	94	
Brazil	69	38	49	76	65
Bulgaria *	70	30	40	85	
China *	80	20	66	30	118
Colombia	67	13	64	80	
Czech Republic *	57	58	57	74	13
Denmark	18	74	16	23	
Estonia *	40	60	30	60	
Finland	33	63	26	59	
France	68	71	43	86	
Germany	35	67	66	65	31
Greece	60	35	57	112	
Hungary *	46	80	88	82	50
India	77	48	56	40	61
Ireland	28	70	68	35	
Israel	13	54	47	81	
Italy	50	76	70	75	
Japan	54	46	95	92	80
Morocco *	70	46	53	68	
Netherlands	38	80	14	53	44
Norway	31	69	8	50	20
Poland *	68	60	64	93	32
Romania *	90	30	42	90	
Russia *	93	39	36	95	
Slovakia *	104	52	110	51	38

Country	PDI	IDV	MAS	UAI	LTO
South Africa	49	65	63	49	
Spain	57	51	42	86	
Sweden	31	71	5	29	33
Switzerland	34	68	70	58	
Turkey	66	37	45	85	
United Kingdom	35	89	66	35	25
United States	40	91	62	46	29
West Africa	77	20	46	54	16

* Estimated values
** Regional estimated values:
'Arab World' = Egypt, Iraq, Kuwait, Lebanon, Libya, Saudi Arabia, United Arab Emirates
'East Africa' = Ethiopia, Kenya, Tanzania, Zambia
'West Africa' = Ghana, Nigeria, Sierra Leone

Cultural questionnaire

Section 1 Where do you feel more comfortable?

Children should be taught that their opinion is as important as their parents	1 2 3 4 5	Children should be taught to never question their parents' authority
Children should be taught to not take things for granted, in the family or other institutions	1 2 3 4 5	Children should be taught to accept the authority of older or important people
In a company/organization, people must be able to create their own place/function	1 2 3 4 5	All people in an organization or company have clearly defined roles
People must not take the boss decisions for granted. Always question the actions of the boss.	1 2 3 4 5	The boss takes all decisions, everybody in a organization/company accept and respect him
The most effective way to change a political system is through public debates and free elections	1 2 3 4 5	The most effective way to change a political system is to replace those in power through drastic means
TOTAL		

Section 2 Where do you feel more comfortable?

People have strong loyalty to the group(s) they belong to	1 2 3 4 5	People choose their friends based on common likes/dislikes/interests
The conventions/rules of the group I belong to influence my behavior	1 2 3 4 5	I have full personal freedom
I am concerned with what the others think about me	1 2 3 4 5	I am concerned only with my own rules and objectives
People are promoted/recognized based on their loyalty and age	1 2 3 4 5	People are promoted based on competence, no matter their age
It is immoral for a boss not to offer a job to a relative	1 2 3 4 5	It is immoral for a boss to offer a job to a relative
TOTAL		

Section 3 Where do you feel more comfortable?

I have sympathy for those who do not win and I envy others for their success	1 2 3 4 5	I admire winners and think those who lose must be punished
At work, I am motivated by a relaxed, friendly atmosphere	1 2 3 4 5	At work, I need to have clear objectives and an evaluation system for what I accomplish
Decisions at work must be based on consensus	1 2 3 4 5	Conflict is positive and productive
A good quality of life is important for both men and women	1 2 3 4 5	Men should be focused on material success and women must be concerned with the well-being of others
I seek love and mutual affection in a partner	1 2 3 4 5	What I want most from my partner is support in difficult situations
TOTAL		

Section 4 Where do you feel more comfortable?

Children must be taught to cope with chaos and ambiguity	1 2 3 4 5	Children must be taught to be organized and avoid ambiguity
People who can move in different environments are appreciated in society	1 2 3 4 5	High competence and expert leadership are appreciated in society
People should always have to carry an ID	1 2 3 4 5	People should always have an ID
It is improper to express feelings in public	1 2 3 4 5	It is ok to show feelings in public, at the right place and time
Society has very few rules	1 2 3 4 5	There are some rules and customs that all people must respect
TOTAL		

Section 5 Where do you feel more comfortable?

People know very clearly what is Good and what is Bad	1 2 3 4 5	People embark on common goals without being so concerned with what is Good and what is Bad
People value personal stability and continuity	1 2 3 4 5	People think everything is relative and permanently changing
Children must be taught to ask WHY	1 2 3 4 5	Children must be taught to ask WHAT and HOW
People's behaviour is always influenced by their roots	1 2 3 4 5	People project their actions into the future
People want coherence in the information they are presented	1 2 3 4 5	People can live with contradictory information
TOTAL		

APPENDIX 5

Publication Transcendental Love Journal

ALBERTO I. VARGAS GONZALO ALONSO-BASTARRECHE DAAN VAN SCHALKWIJK

Transcendence and Love for a New Global Society

PROCEEDINGS OF THE II INTERNATIONAL CONGRESS TRANSCENDENCE AND LOVE FOR A NEW GLOBAL SOCIETY (WARSAW, AUGUST 1–2, 2016)

CO-ORGANIZED BY:

INTERNATIONAL ASSOCIATION FOR PHILOSOPHICAL ANTHROPOLOGY (WASHINGTON, D.C., USA)

CENTRE FOR THE THOUGHT OF JOHN PAUL II (WARSAW, POLAND)

LEONARDO POLO INSTITUTE OF PHILOSOPHY (CHICAGO, IL, USA)

Cuadernos de Pensamiento Espanol

CUADERNOS DE PENSAMIENTO ESPANOL

CONSEJO EDITORIAL

ISBN: 978-84-8081-526-0
Deposito Legal: NA 0252-2017
Pamplona

Nº 64: Alberto I. Vargas / Gonzalo Alonso-Bastarreche / Daan Van Schalkwijk (eds.), *Transcendence and Love for a New Global Society* 2017

© Alberto I. Vargas / Daan Van Schalkwijk / Gonzalo Alonso-Bastarreche

CUADERNOS DE PENSAMIENTO ESPANOL SERVICIO DE PUBLICACIONES DE LA UNIVERSIDAD DE NAVARRA. S. A.

31080 Pamplona. Tfn.: 948 42 56 00. Fax: 948 42 56 36
Ulzama digital, s. l., Pol. Ind. Areta. Huarte
calle A-33. 31620 Huarte (Navarra)

Table of Contents

Notes

INSPIRING THE *SENSE OF VOCATION* IN FUTURE BUSINESS LEADERS THROUGH CHARACTER EDUCATION

Claudio Andres Rivera[1]

Abstract

For more than 100 years, business leaders have been traditionally educated in business schools, which generally have influenced decisively the what, how, and why of their profession. The latest financial crises and corporate scandals, particularly the 2008 crisis, have promoted a revision of the role, approach, and curricula of business school programs. Major initiatives have been launched all across the globe, for example, the United Nation PRME program. They have encouraged the incorporation of more ethical values in the management and teaching activities of business schools.

However, most of these initiatives have been limited simply to the incorporation of new tools and reporting activities. Though these new tools are helping students and professors to look at business *beyond the financial bottom line*, they have so far failed to help students and professors to understand the deeper ethical meaning of the business world. In this sense, one the limiting paradigms is the one that considers *business school* simply a professional school with a prioritization of the teaching of *useful content*. This paradigm prevents the incorporation of content and approaches, which could help students to understand better the ethical and anthropological roots of their profession.

I will elaborate on these issues in the paper and will propose the promotion of the concept of *character education* as a suitable vehicle for the general re-introduction of ethical and anthropological content in business schools. The author argues that this strategy could support the inspiration of the *sense of vocation* between business schools students and could help anthropology be seen as *more relevant* for business schools.

---

[1] *Research Assistants:* Oscar Pau Vinaixa and Guillermo Mislata Correa (University of Navarre).

Introduction: Role of Business Schools and the Formation of Leaders

In a society powered by its economy and a mechanistic vision of the human being, it is more needed than ever that business schools—the *crib* of managers, entrepreneurs, and business leaders—take the responsibility for educating leaders who display a broad and deep view of the person and the society, who understand the meaning of the economy, and who are motivated not only for their own interest, in other words, exclusively for their profit. In other words, we need that business schools educate leaders with a deep sense of the meaning of their profession. It means that they see their business profession as a calling, a vocation.

If the mentors of the business schools forget the essential and focus mainly on the *superficial*, this attitude will hinder the long-term perspective so needed for exercising business responsibly. Missing the long-term will leave a void in the value systems of individuals and negatively impact their character. A person's character is built of habits that require a set of intellectual convictions or values. If business schools focus on the short term, the expected holistic education of the reality of business will become narrowed to utilitarianism. In this way, business schools might easily become simply the *channels of communication* toward *generally accepted ideas*—a place where faculty delivers *acceptable ideas*, not where information becomes knowledge.

To educate future leaders, business schools need to personalize their education as, in order to work in their values and deepest assumptions, they need to make an effort to understand each individual, the personal reality of each student. In this way, schools can become more efficient in appealing directly to each individual and leave their mere divulgate function in order to become more knowledge enhancers.

Learning impacts the appreciation students have of themselves. This makes the work of business school educators harder. Education is about truth, and truth often means giving up on things and perspectives, which are stable in the mindset of the students. Hence, if the student wants to learn, he needs to have the willingness to recognize his own needs and failures.

The business schools face many challenges regarding of programs: identity, faculty, environment, and the variety of demands from the different stakeholders. But, the most significant challenge is to *awake* an authentic willingness to learn among the students.

In my experience, on the one hand, most students come to business schools to upgrade their technical knowledge and further build their network. On the other, and sometimes primarily, they come to a business school to understand or find a vision and mission for their future career. Managers see a difference between who they are and who they think they should be. Their implicit or explicit objective in business school is many times to close this gap. Closing this gap implies a big investment in self-awareness, which schools many times do not have the capacity to undertake.

If business schools do not take their role in the formation process of business leaders seriously, and they just focus themselves in the distribution of generally accepted ideas, they run the risk of losing the trust of their communities and their leaders. That happens already, unfortunately. And, there is certain reason for this claim. Many consider that business schools do not manage to send the right message or they do not send it in the right way.

The role of a business school is nothing less than giving to men the possibility to reach their full potential, meanwhile they exercise an administrative function. Hence, schools should first deliver a deep vision of human problems and then teach management skills. You cannot sail a boat without expertise with the scoreboard. In the same sense, you cannot guide people without knowing who the human being is. If we train people with the wrong assumptions, then we will not help them in leading organizations.

Business organizations are integrated by people; therefore, it is very difficult to control them and their destiny. Once we understand people, we learn that they will not always take the most logical and linear path. Hence, business schools should leave behind not such real theories, and teach future leaders instead what human nature is and the meaning of business activity.

The Concept of Human Being in Business Schools

Business schools play a fundamental role in creating the concept of *business* that leaders have. This concept ends up as a determining factor of the behavior, which is considered adequate for the development of business activity. This influence of business schools in the business world is not at all identical everywhere. Organizations themselves, of course, influence the understanding of the reality of business. However, business schools are the key players to foster values and ideas that enhance adequate behaviors in the people who might become leaders and executives.

The recent economic crises have stressed the concern regarding the role that businesses play inside their communities.[2] Their activity, besides the fact of being exclusively private, has an enormous impact on the whole of the society. Businesses are not only places of creation of employment and offers of services, they have become the principal agent for the management of the world's resources, both natural and human. Therefore, any change in the way business schools approach education will not just impact business organizations but also all the stakeholders. At least in the short term, the bankruptcy of a business creates a much bigger effect than a wrong political decision.

All family and politics will depend to a large extent on how organizations run their internal life. This is a call to no longer miss the social character of any business organization. The social character of the firm cannot be avoided anymore. Recent financial crises exposed the consequences of companies, whose aims are not directed toward the common good. An irresponsible management style produces prejudice not only to the firm itself but also to many other stakeholders.[3] These visible consequences triggered a more fluid discussion on the significance of responsible management.

Business schools have been embedded with the predominant ideologies of the last century: individualism and utilitarianism—both are at the end two sides of the same coin.[4] Given that profit has been always positioned as the fundamental and primary goal of any firm, all other objectives have been subjected to that. Maximizing shareholder value has been always considered the single most important evaluation criteria for managers. All this clearly states that other initially fundamental duties such as the quality of service provided to the community and the development of the workforce have never been top criteria for measuring success in business. In this way, the human capital became a mean for the

---

[2] O'Connell, M. and L. Sweeney. 2015. "An Action Plan for Implementing the Principles for Responsible Management Education in College of Business Progamme Learning Outcomes." *DIT Teaching Fellowship Reports,* 2014–2015.

[3] Sison, A.J.G., and J. Fontrodona. 2012. "The Common Good of the Firm in the Aristotelian-Thomistic Tradition." *Business Ethics Quarterly* 22. pp. 211–246.

[4] Mele, D. 2013. "Antecedents and Current Situation of Humanistic Management." *African Journal of Business Ethics* 7, no. 2. pp. 10–19.

maximization of profits as any other resource. It is apparent that such an approach can generate serious problems. When there is no connection between the well-being of the person, of the community, and of the business, the conflict of interest will just naturally emanate.

Obvious challenges arise: should business benefit fit shareholders or society? What is the goal of profit? Is it not clear that profit is purely an instrumental reality rather than an honorable aim serving a larger goal? How should those involved in business activities benefit from them in terms of personal development? Individualism, the loss of the notion of person and common good, ends up making human relations just a means for achieving material ends rather than personal growth.

There are, though, trends toward the fostering of a more human vision of business. This *more human side* is justified mainly from a utilitarian perspective: if we want sustainable growth, we need quality in human relationships. The idea of *the firm* as a mean toward more fundamental objectives is shared neither in practice nor in theory. Many of the failures of the business community are connected with this misunderstanding of the role of business. We can observe even problems in social development as poverty and different forms of slavery.[5]

Besides utilitarianism, an individualistic vision of man prevails. Individualism stresses the satisfaction of the individual's own needs above the ones of the community. The community is *attached* to man and social relations are considered instrumental for achieving exclusively individual goals. The community becomes a *distribution system* of individual goods, and human relations are subjected to a system that excludes through individual possession. Holding something implies that someone else is excluded of it. Departing from here, citizens consider that their own achievement of a certain good implies others' exclusion of this good. The ideal of *shared value* is deemed as unviable. This deep split of goods is at the end the understanding of the social phenomenon as a result of a contract where the individual interest is the foundation stone. With all this said, it is clear that in this concept of business, other individuals are mainly instrument for the achievement of my own good.[6]

If we look at the reality of the firm, it all implies to decontextualize the business reality, narrowing it down to the production of profit just

---

[5] Ibid.

[6] Sison, A.J.G., and J. Fontrodona. 2011. "The Common Good of Business: Addressing a Challenge Posed by Caritas in Veritate." *Journal of Business Ethics* 100, no. 1, pp. 99–107.

for profit. If there is not common good, there is no reason to subordinate one's own interest for the sake of others' interest. Why should I care about social well-being if it does not add to my financial wealth? The business or the individual will do what produces a benefit and only that.

Given these philosophical principles—utilitarianism and individualism—there is not room for doing things beyond our own interests. Given that we understand man as individual, other or others do not have relevance in the development and fulfillment of human nature. Only in understanding the human being as a person, and then as a relational being, does the quality of the human relations appear as an opportunity for growth and plenitude of human nature.

An Anthropological Proposal

If our main objective is to shape an anthropological foundation of business, we should start from the most basic of the anthropological principles: *man is a person and, therefore, the author, center, and end of all social and economic life.* Hence, we cannot speak about the anthropological foundation of business, without discussing first its main source: the person. For example, if we say that the businessman is the one who mobilizes the business world, *businessman* will firstly have a human meaning follow by a professional one. As a consequence, due to the fact that we talk about the *businessman* first as a person and then as a business-person, the ethical meaning of his work will have a renewed significance.

Man has plurality of dimensions. This plurality does not mean dualism, but rather, duality as these dimensions are different realities in terms of relevance, but they do not oppose each other. Moreover, these realities need each other.[7] [8]

Business activity is in itself a human dimension, a human dimension that complements itself with others. This dimension has a certain position

---

[7] Benedicto XVI, *Caritas in Veritate,* from: http://w2.vatican.va/content/benedictxvi/es/ency- clicals/documents/hf_ben-xvi_enc_20090629_caritas-in-veritate.html

[8] *J. F. Selles,* Los tres agentes del cambio en la Sociedad civil, *Tribuna siglo XXI, Madrid 2013.*

in relationship to other dimensions, and it needs others in order to gain understanding of its significance. It is clear then that an *homo economicus* vision of the human being—an underlying assumption in business education—where everything in man is directed toward the maximization of business profit is at least primitive as it forgets the vision of man as composed of a plurality of dimensions.

The most radical human dimension and the basis of all others is the distinction between *being and essence.* The act of being is the very same human person, his personal intimacy. The essence is composed of reason and will. The act of being is superior to the essence as we are capable of perfecting reason and will. Man is more than his reason and will. This distinction proves that it makes sense of the existence of order between different human dimensions. Understanding Leonardo Polo's dimension of the act of being will clarify the significance of the business dimension of man.

The act of being is conformed by four transcendentals: personal love, personal knowledge, personal freedom, and personal coexistence. These are not things that the human being has in terms of possession, they are rather aspects of who the man is.

The first transcendental is personal love. This the first and the one, which describes the best the human person. All other transcendentals are subordinated to this one. We are not talking about a potency, we are talking about an act, the act of love, the love that overflows, and whose most authentic manifestation is *to give* and to give something that is superior to everything else.[9]

Human love is constituted of accepting, giving, and gift. It is all about accepting/giving man as man in order to exercise any of the other human dimensions. Hence, we cannot accept/give the human dimension of business without first accepting man as a person. Furthermore, man cannot give if he is not welcomed first and if he does not accept to be welcomed first. Man can only give as long as he accepts to be welcomed. Lastly, we have *the gift*; man can only offer gifts as long as he gives first himself to others. The gift is just a thing and therefore the last dimension of the transcendental of love.

---

[9] Ibid.

The second transcendental is personal knowledge, and it implies basically the awareness of our own personal meaning. There cannot be personal acceptance if there is not first personal knowledge. There cannot be acceptance by others if we are not first accepted by ourselves. We do not give to others what we do not know or we do not accept first. Without self-giving, gifts become scarce, and therefore, the natural order of man gets broken. Personal love falls short as it cannot plainly do what is proper of itself, that is, *to give*.[10]

The third transcendental is human freedom. This is the basis of ethics, as without freedom, there would not be choice, and without choice, there would not be room to choose behavior. We would end up in determinism and the consequent negation of ethics. Furthermore, without capacity of choice, there would not be human work, as it would imply the denial of choosing a personal way of production of wealth. Without human work, there would not be a business world.

The last transcendental is personal coexistence. This implies the opening of each human person to his own intimacy. This implies that every person is potentially open to his own intimacy, to his deepest meaning and being. However, no one can be alone, not even in his deepest intimacy. We need others to be. Analogically, an isolated person is not the unit of the business world, but rather the person who coexists with others, therefore an organization.

After outlining the four transcendentals, we can position business activity as a natural reality in each man. A man is in his very roots a being who acts *in* business—not a being who acts *for* business. As man is a being who gives, he has the capacity to offer gifts. If work would not exist, there would not be a business world, and without a business world, man could not continue *giving*, as work means essentially *to give*. Man gives because he is capable of more, he is not satisfy just receiving.

Summarizing and simplifying, managers should understand the human transcendental, as the business world is conformed by persons who are essentially lovers, aware of themselves, free, and need to coexist with others. Without understanding man, managers cannot develop their

---

[10] Ibid.

organizations fully.[11] The business-person should start understanding who is firstly himself and who are *the others*. In a way, he needs to progressively know the proper personal meaning of each person of the organization. He should grasp as well the common nature of all men—the natural law— and how it could be perfected.[12]

Regarding freedom, a good leader knows that freedom and motivation—and ultimately productivity—correlate. The more free a business-person is, the more likely that he will manage to insert more meaning in his decisions. Further, the more free his workers are, the more he can guarantee personal initiative in the fulfillment of his decisions. If the person that manages, promotes his subordinates more, they will do things with more freedom and, therefore, with more responsibility.[13]

Finally, we want to call into consideration that, given that a person becomes fully himself *giving*, the content and beneficiaries of the gifts are important. The more humanizing the content of the gift is and as more people can accept the gift, the more personal development will occur. A consequence is that a business activity, in order to become humanly enriching, cannot provide benefit to just a "few", to just the shareholders. Any business activity should create positive change in the whole society. Then, society as a beneficiary of the business activity becomes essential for making business meaningful.[14]

Wrapping up: business activity is a real dimension of man, and exists, thanks to the pre-existence of him. Man can make business meaningful if he knows himself and knows his very nature. All this requires anthropological expertise, which allows leaders and employees to understand the very nature of business activity and work. Character education as an appropriate vehicle for introducing a more adequate anthropology.

Observing the reality of man is a fascinating though arduous task. In the context of experimental sciences, things are much simpler, as the material world is their object. Experimental sciences have a solid

---

[11] *Leonardo Polo*, Quien es el hombre, Obras Completas Volumen X. *Eunsa, Pamplona, 2016.*

[12] J. Fernando Selles, *op. cit.*

[13] Ibid.

[14] Ibid.

cornerstone: the principle of causality. Through the principle of causality, they can establish necessary and predictable natural laws. Human reality is different. How can we draw necessary and predictable laws of behavior of a being, whose fundamental characteristic is freedom? When studying human behavior, either we avoid the ambition of controlling this object or we end up pretending results.[15]

If there is freedom, not everything can be determined by law. The act of being of man is radically different from the rest of the created universe.[16] Because he is free, he attributes meaning to everything he does. The direction of his life is ultimately the result of the accumulation of his decisions. These decisions sometimes may be driven partially by the trivial or unexpected, but freedom will give them always the dynamic of decision–action rather than cause–effect.[17]

Therefore, the study of human behavior will be different than the study of nature. Needless to say, the different dimensions of the human being will require inputs from branches other than philosophy. So, our claim is not one of isolation of the humanistic sciences from experimental sciences. Rather, in order to understand the human being, an interdisciplinary approach will be needed.

One of the most crucial distinctions between human being and the rest of the universe and that has a determinant consequence in social sciences, including business, is the following: the universe is a useful thing, man is absolutely useless. The universe is for man. Each element in nature has an assigned role and a function amidst the whole universe. The human being is completely different. The human being does not seek to adapt to the environment, he adapts the environment to his needs.[18] The existence of man is not conditioned by nature. He is an end in himself, and his main concern is his own development. His own development is

---

[15] Ghoshal, S. 2005. "Bad Management Theories Are Destroying Good Management Practices." *Academy of Management Learning & Education* 4, no. 1, pp. 75–91.

[16] Polo, L. 2016. Presente y futuro del hombre, Obras Completas Volumen X. *Eunsa, Pamplona.*

[17] Tomas de Aquino, *Summa Theologiae*, I-II, q. 1.

[18] L. Polo, *Quien es el hombre*, ed. cit.

simply to seek his plenitude as man, and all his behavior is in this sense ethical: it helps or restrains his own ultimate fulfillment.

Summing up: man seeks fundamentally and freely his own fulfilment. And, he does it with full personal responsibility, deciding why and whom. Using plainly this responsibility makes the man full of life. Every man has a life that is expecting to be lived, not external causes will decide for him. This indetermination, in certain way, leaves man in a situation of risk. The life of every man, independent of the context, is essentially risky because it depends on the way how he exercises freedom. Hence, a learning process is not so much about understanding the context as how to *drive the context* according to our needs.[19]

Education is, then, primarily a gateway to our own world. Its relevance is not connected simply with its scientific–technical side. Its relevance is fundamentally connected with the heart of man, his capacity and clarity for decision, his character. The main object of education is man. All other objects are subordinated, as they just constitute instruments for achieving the main goal: the fulfillment of man, the perfecting of his character.[20] The *value* of money is connected only and exclusively with its function of acquiring other goods and of bringing support for carrying out projects or activities. The end goal of these other goods and activities are decided by man and depend on the level of awareness of his own needs.

Given all that has been aforementioned, we can dig deeper on the content of education. If man is fundamentally free and he is not subjected to the determination of things, education should be the education of freedom. Then, education cannot be narrowed simply to *means*, but it should reach the consideration of the aims. Choosing the right aims and how to achieve them demands learning and training. At the end, any person does what he knows and will.

If the objective of life is a good life, to be happy, accomplishing it requires understanding how to reach it.[21] In order to know how, we need

---

[19] Ibid.

[20] Benedicto XVI, *Caritas in Veritate*, 26.

[21] Aristotle. 1984. "Nicomachean Ethics" In *The Complete Works of Aristotle, Volume 2,* ed. Barnes, J. The Revised Oxford Translation. Princeton University Press, Princeton, N.J.

first to know who. And, here we come to one of the most challenged principles in modern history: if it is true that man sets his own objectives, man
is not fully autonomous, as he is in himself given. Humanity is given, and
this is the fundamental point of departure. Therefore, education is not
so much about creating a destiny as discovering man to man. Education
should help man to become adapted to himself, to do what is good for
himself, and this should be appealing to reason and will, in a word to
character.[22] Character is, therefore, the most determinant factor of our
behavior. If character is educated, man will do what is good for him.
Man will like what he should like and will have clarity on what is right.
In education, it is important that man develops the right taste for what
brings him to plenitude.

An education of character requires a holistic approach. A person exercises his character everywhere and in everything. The human life is not
composed of a mosaic of disconnected realities. Instead, the life of man is
one single project, which is comprehensive. Further, the different realities
of the life of a person contributes or restrain his own development. His
behavior in private will impact his behavior in public and vice versa. Man
is always committed toward what he seeks; he identifies himself with his
own aims. This is the reason that man acquires an identity with his own
actions. All human behavior has a subjective consequence beyond the
external consequences.

The will, even when has many concrete and small manifestations,
owes its operation to the last willed end.[23] Man always and in everything
acts according to his last will. If man wills a fulfilled life, his life will be a
continuous acting toward reaching fulfillment. When education forgets
that man is one and our life is only one, or that our behavior impacts our
way of being, education misses the fundamentals of our person or mixes
up the order of our personal reality. All this has determinant consequences
for business education. An education process of a business-person will be
incomplete and even delusional if it avoids dealing with his private life
and his personal development.[24]

---

[22] Tomas de Aquino, *Summa Theologiae*, I–II, q. 49.
[23] Tomas de Aquino, *Summa Theologiae*, I–II, q. 10.
[24] Benedicto XVI, *Caritas in Veritate*, 51.

Business education should primarily address character education, as it approaches the development of each person in all its integrity and recognizes that man as a free being needs to be educated on understanding and willing what is good. Character education is more effective than ethical education. Ethics will teach what is good and will primarily appeal to reason. Character education will educate not only the reason but also the will. Man will not do good just because he knows that is good, he will because *knowing he will it.*[25]

Conclusions

The fact that character education starts to be heard in the business world, though still in a marginal way, is a good sign. It means at least that there is a higher awareness of the moral nature of business activity. In a firm, people do not only produce goods, but there is a *human side*, which cannot be avoided. The work of the business-person goes beyond the productive and physical limits: it impacts the whole society, the employees, the business-person himself. The firm is not, therefore, an isolated entity. On the contrary, it is an institution that, amidst the social net, fulfills a very important function: it is the place of the personal fulfillment of all its members and the principal provider and manager of wealth.[26]

A large part of the global population spends a substantial time of their lives in business organizations. They devote and invest most of their talents in the goals of these entities. It is obvious, then, that the need that these organizations become an opportunity for personal growth and fulfillment. The firm becomes then one of the most fundamental places for exercising of each person's vocation. The firm can help each person to find a meaning for his life if the firm's underlying philosophy—there is always one!—approaches decisively the development of each person from the development of his character. If a person can use business life as an opportunity to grow in character, then business life becomes *useful* for achieving fulfillment in life.

---

[25] D. Goleman, *Inteligencia emocional,* Kairos, Barcelona, 1996.

[26] A. J. G. Sison and J. Fontrodona, *op. cit.*

We need to underline here again that business life is a human activity, and as such, is subordinated to other more fundamental dimensions of man. Business life is useful as long as it serves the whole of man. Of course, there is an objective content in business, but this is not exclusive. The subjective content of business and work is the impact that business and work has in the person who does it.

Hence, character education, it means the education of reason and will that allows people to exercise for his own good his freedom, should be a fundamental component of business education. In this way, business education will leave aside a vision of business-person, which presents him as fragmented. Only one is the person who lives in and out business. Only one is the ultimate objective of life in and out business. Therefore, there is not a basis to consider business an amoral activity, meaning an activity disconnected from man's last aim: personal happiness.

Many challenges are ahead of a proposal of full integration of character education in business education. One is to make the participants to understand the intertwined relationship of business and life. Understanding that we can and must be happy working in business is fundamental. Avoiding narrowed and fragmented views of business activity can help the students to understand the role of their business life in the context of their lives. This triggers the understanding that the firm can improve (or harm) our own life and the lives of others. This vision will foster the *sense of vocation*, the sense of the call of being a business-person. To give, a constitutive element of personal being, finds in the firm the institution through which we can give our talents in a privileged context[27].

Being father, brother, member of a community is all perfectly compatible with being a business-person. To foster character education is a good strategy to grow on the understanding of an idea of the firm, which is integrated with the rest of the institutions where the person is. In the large extent, to make work and business activity an opportunity to improve our humanity depends on the solidity of character education as nobody can exercise what he does not know. With character education will come along other currently popular ideas: social responsibility, broad

---

[27] *L. Polo,* Quien es el hombre.

vision, work–life balance, critical thinking, innovation. It is hard for a business-person to become a driver of the organization if he lacks the strength of will and reason, which strong character provides.

Extra Bibliography

Pablo VI. Vaticano II. Constitution pastoral *Gaudium et Spes* sobre la iglesia en el mundo actual. Dic 7 de 1965. From: http://vatican.va/archive/-hist_councils/ii_vatican_council/documents/vat-ii_const_19651207_gau-dium-et-spes_sp.html

Claudio Andres Rivera

Associate Professor

RTU Riga Business School

APPENDIX 6

Best Self-Portrait
Best Practices

Excellent

Because no special layout requirements were set for this paper, I decided to use this opportunity and write the intro before I pass any tests identifying strengths and talents or ask anyone's opinion.

What I wanted to do first was take a moment and think on my strong sides without any biases. While I always saw myself as a positive thinker (which could be the first of worthy traits), it turned out that I see my own faults much clearer than positive traits, even when trying to concentrate on the strengths. Whenever I think on a strong side, I can find the case when this trait has not worked so well. So, probably self-criticism or self-objectivity is another good trait. One more moment that comes to my mind is an intention to treat people in a good way and be a good person. Flexibility is a trait that can be considered as a positive as well.

These are the personality tones that are most obvious to me, but now I would like to take some tests and talk to my boss, subordinate, and boyfriend to understand whether what I see is similar to what is seen by others. These three people were chosen, because they are in touch with me on a daily basis. The interviews were hold in an informal way, where interviewees were allowed to talk without any mentioning of tests results or other *spoilers* or influences from my side.

So, let us take a look at the results I received (similar traits are marked in the same colors):

The correlation of my own vision with opinion of others shows that all the traits I have defined initially are mentioned by interviewees as well. So, I have no illusions about myself. In the meantime, it is really pleasant to

Own vision versus other sources

Own vision	Authentic Happiness Tests (VIA Survey of Character Strengths, Brief Strengths Test, The Grit Survey)	Company MD (direct supervisor)	Subordinate	Boyfriend
Positive thinker	Appreciation of beauty and excellence	Ability to see the full picture (perfect accomplishment, even if only general information or direction is given, not a detailed task)	Intuition (always know what exactly is the best action in any situation)	Beautiful
Self-criticism/self-objectivity	Judgment, critical thinking, open-mindedness	Ability to work independently, without being controlled	Logic, practical, rational thinking (ability to handle even finance issues)	Ready to help
Treating people in a good way (efforts to be a good person)	Creativity, ingenuity, originality	Precision and fast working pace	Pathfinder, explorer (compared to Columbus)—looking for new challenges and fresh ideas to try	Sincere and honest
Flexibility—meaning ability to operate in different circumstances, communicate with different people, even if I do not like it that much	Forgiveness and mercy	Rational thinking and understanding of technologies combined with creativity (both figures and art, which is rare and valuable combination)	Sophistication, good taste, quality and femininity	Sensitive
	Kindness and generosity	Reliable (no need for reminders, everything will be done in time and in a good manner)		Fun, interesting to be with

Passion for long-term goals (suggestion to accomplish very difficult challenges)		Optimistic
	Work and time management, priority setting (huge work flow, but high efficiency; able to manage lots of things)	
	Open and friendly (ability to communicate with people in a pleasant way, with empathy, respecting others)	Generous, Kind
		Responsible
		Modest
		Polite

find out that the most commonly mentioned strengths are related to my intention to be nice to people, which means that I succeed in that direction.

Another great surprise is the fact that other people and tests showed much more positive feedbacks about me than I could come up with myself. Some things seemed natural and for granted (e.g., appreciation of beauty and excellence, forgiveness and mercy, reliability, responsibility, honesty), while they turned out to be very important at work and in personal life. Moreover, I found out that some traits I always perceived more as cons are highly appreciated and evaluated by people around me (modesty, sensitivity, sometimes excessive politeness). On top of that, I noticed that my vision of myself may differ from day to day (depending on the mood, success of hair stylist, presence of the sun, and other factors), while others see me more or less the same.

It is also curious to take a closer look on how vision is different by type of my relationships with interviewees (please refer to the following table). Of course, my boyfriend is the one who knows me the best from personal point of view, which is the reason why he mentioned personal traits only. In the meantime, people from working environment focus more on business issues. Still, it is obvious that some personal pros are relevant for working processes as well. Besides, these qualities differ depending on working relationships type (e.g., being friendly and responsible—is important for supervisor, being creative and sophisticated—for subordinate). On top of that, the same traits are seen differently by different people: appreciation of beauty is the same as sophistication, good taste, and even sensitivity, while responsibility in combination with honesty may be perceived as reliability. Unexpectedly, the most frequently mentioned talent is creativity, which I supposed was the part of my job responsibilities as a marketing person.

As a result, it is clear to me that I am much better person than I could even imagine. It is nice to know that people around me are ready to find time to support me (even MD agreed to free some time in a tight schedule for the interview and discussion needed to prepare this paper). Even more, they see me as a good person and valuable colleague.

The idea of what my strengths are was occupying my mind for some time already, but I never succeeded to find the answers until today.

Differences by source of information

Own vision	Authentic Happiness Tests (VIA Survey of Character Strengths, Brief Strengths Test, The Grit Survey)	Company MD (direct supervisor)	Subordinate	Boyfriend
Positive thinker	Appreciation of beauty and excellence	Ability to see the full picture (perfect accomplishment, even if only general information or direction is given, not a detailed task)	Intuition (always know what exactly is the best action in any situation)	Beautiful
Self-criticism/self-objectivity	Judgment, critical thinking, open-mindedness	Ability to work independently, without being controlled	Logic, practical, rational thinking (ability to handle even finance issues)	Ready to help
Treating people in a good way (efforts to be a good person)	Creativity, ingenuity, originality	Precision and fast working pace	Pathfinder, explorer (compared to Columbus)—looking for new challenges and fresh ideas to try	Sincere and honest
Flexibility—meaning ability to operate in different circumstances, communicate with different people, even if I do not like it that much	Forgiveness and mercy	Rational thinking and understanding of technologies combined with creativity (both figures and art, which is rare and valuable combination)	Sophistication, good taste, quality and femininity	Sensitive

(Continued)

Continued

Own vision	Authentic Happiness Tests (VIA Survey of Character Strengths, Brief Strengths Test, The Grit Survey)	Company MD (direct supervisor)	Subordinate	Boyfriend
	Kindness and generosity	Reliable (no need for reminders, everything will be done in time and in a good manner)		Fun, interesting to be with
	Passion for long-term goals (suggestion to accomplish very difficult challenges)	Work and time management, priority setting (huge work flow, but high efficiency; able to manage lots of things)		Optimistic
		Open and friendly (ability to communicate with people in a pleasant way, with empathy, respecting others)		Generous/ kind
				Responsible
				Modest
				Polite

This task definitely helped me to analyze myself, focusing on the positive traits, and finally, I can see that there are reasons to be proud of myself and go further with even more positive expectations and be grateful. In fact, now I am more confident than ever and see the direction for both personal and career development in future.

I guess the best conclusion might be the quote of my supervisor: "You have no right to be so humble about your strength, because you have really convincing reasons to be proud of yourself." All the feedbacks I received, including this one, were worth given exercise to be fulfilled!

PS: Here is the visualization of my strengths:

Good

From an early age, I have always been developing and acting on ideas. I would say that I am not the traditional entrepreneur; I like to consider myself more as an ideas addict. I am always armed with my notepad rather than an iPad, constantly jotting down ideas and brainstorming.

I get a feeling of excitement when sharing ideas and mapping out plans with other people. In the development stages, I often get in a bit of a zone, potentially even slightly over excitable, but this passion and energy often rubs off on to other people. During the developmental stages, I am quite introverted, but during the sharing stages, I am very much extraverted. The sensation of appreciation and support gives me a real fillip, and the energy to give it a shot!!

I remember, at my 21st birthday celebrations, my father stated to close friends and family that I tend to live life on the edge. I think this is a fair observation to sum up my attitude while taking on new challenges and seizing on opportunities. This is the main reason why I chose the path to work for myself and be an entrepreneur.

I am a great believer in the power of the mind. I often refer to this poem when I feel not so confident and doubtful of my abilities and need a kick up the backside. It inspires me to *think differently* and adopt new approaches to help me overcome moments of difficulty in life:

If you think you are beaten, you are,

If you think you dare not, you don't.

If you like to win, but you think you can't,

It is almost certain you won't.

If you think you'll lose, you're lost,

For out in the world we find,

Success begins with a fellow's will.

It's all in the state of mind.

If you think you are outclassed, you are,

You've got to think high to rise,

You've got to be sure of yourself before

You can ever win a prize.

Life's battles don't always go

To the stronger or faster man.

But soon or late the man who wins,

Is the man who thinks he can.

~ C. W. Longenecker ~

Creativity is the secret to my success in being able to develop ideas and think intuitively. At school, I enjoyed my fine art course, and I know when I find the time to paint time seems to fly by. Again, I fall back into the zone!! This is the case when working in any creative form, whether it is making films, brainstorming, designing concepts, photographing; I like to think I can offer a creative edge and mindset to almost anything. Before moving to Latvia, I was working in schools assisting teachers to teach traditional subjects such as geography, history, math, etc. in a creative way, using with film, painting, or drama. A colleague once gave me the feedback "working with you Aus, I learnt that business can be creative." I will never forget, this and I always try to encourage those I associate with and manage to be creative and intuitive in their work; it certainly makes it more fun and enjoyable!

I am fairly sensitive and responsive to other people's feelings and concerns; I have a high sense of emotional intelligence. I always try to see the positives and strengths in other people's personalities and can get frustrated at times when they do not utilize them to their full potential. I tend to set myself very ambitious targets and others very high expectations of others. This, at times, can cause friction, as more often than not conflicts are caused when expectations are not met, but I have learned to manage this more effectively relatively recently by establishing clearer expectations with people.

This heightened sense of personal intelligence is helping me with my new role as a father. Without a doubt, xxx is the best thing that has ever happened in my life and I am eternal grateful that wife and I have the opportunity to share such a beautiful and rewarding gift. It is so exciting monitoring his development and journey in life!! It also gives you a really deep understanding of what unconditional love is!

Clowning around with xxx is the best hobby anyone could ask for. I suppose this reflects my sense of humor. I am not able to remember and crack a load of jokes, but I often see the funny side and try not to take life too seriously… it is too short after all!! My eccentricness and impulsive outlook to life often creates some attention and laughs as a consequence.

All of my life I have been playing sport. My family is very sporty, and I was fortunate to have the opportunity to play many sports from an early age, both team and individual. Passion, enthusiasm, and eagerness to do my best are virtues I take on to the sports field. I would not say that I am especially gifted at any one particular sport, but I have the ability to learn and play any sport at a reasonable level fairly quickly. I think playing sport has really helped me to become a team player in all walks of life. It teaches you to respect others and a sense of fairness. After all, there is nothing worse than a person who is a *bad sport*.

I am in a period of my life where I need to lead by example. With the birth of my son and being the CEO of xxx, I obviously have more responsibilities than I had when I was 22. With responsibilities does come a sense of pressure. In my childhood, I was not so good at dealing with pressure, I would often get very nervous for exams and not succeeding. This, in some ways, has had a positive impact to always set high expectations and have big ambitions, but I also feel I have found ways to manage pressure more effectively. The RBS Leadership course has certainly helped me manage my thoughts, taught me strategies, and *leveled my persona* in quite a testing period of my life.

This openness and curiosity to learn new skills is the vehicle that has taken me on this exciting journey. Without this eagerness to respond to and also seek new opportunities, I would certainly not be writing this best-self portrait now. I still feel that I am reasonably young at heart, but because of the many experiences and people I have been fortunate to be acquainted with, I would say I have quite a reflective, rounded and wise outlook to life.

But, sometimes, I can overcomplicate life and what it means. Then, I reflect back to a saying that my father once told me. Happiness is like a butterfly: the more you chase it, the more it will elude you. But if you turn your attention to other things, it will come and sit softly on your shoulder.

When playing golf or working on a project, I can find myself simply trying too hard. When this happens, I often try to take a step back, take a deep breath, and compose myself. It is then when the task in hand seems less daunting and achievable. I guess it is a case of being able to rationalize.

I am not particularly religious, but a good friend of the family who is vicar once told me during a very difficult time in my life. "Do to others whatever you would like them to do to you." Should a genie give me one wish I would ask for in this world, I would simply ask him to encourage this philosophy to each and every one of us.

Thank you.

Less Than Good

I have divided my best-self portrait into two parts: professional (related to work) and private (related to out-of-office time).

Professional

As we quite recently (in April) had 360-degree evaluation at work, I already had feedback from my subordinates, colleagues, and superior. Certainly, there were also comments about some necessary improvements. However, in this paper, I will talk only about positive feedback. There will be following structure in this paper: initially I will display some specific comment that people told about me (I will use form *he* because these comments were prepared in written form and sent to the HR department), and then I will provide additional comments and interpretation from my side:

- "He has strong skills of analytical thinking." I would say
  that this is my strongest professional skill that differentiates

me from a lot of other people. It is related both to analysis of numbers and analysis of processes. I can make qualitative analysis and interpretation of different data. I am able to put together a big picture from small pieces and can also divide a big picture to small pieces.

- "He fulfils his duties with all his heart." High level of responsibility also is one of my strongest qualities. If there is a task that I have to accomplish, then I will certainly execute it. I do not need additional motivation for this. Even if needed, then I will find some internal motivation because it is my responsibility and I have to do this. I do not like to disappoint people who rely on me.

- "He is a competent person in his area, knowledgeable and constructive." I chose sphere of activity where I knew that I can provide good results and constantly I improve my skills and knowledge that also helps improving professional results. For example, despite having one master's degree, I am studying at RBS and going for second master's degree.

- "He is leading his department close to an excellence." I know that I am as good leader as good is my team. Thus, I invest my time in order to develop my subordinates and increase their professional skills. Also, I organize different out-of-office events in order to strengthening collaboration between all team members.

- "He is precise and almost never make mistakes." I am accurate and always double-check data if they are important. Thus, I can avoid mistakes and people trust that information, which will be provided from my side, always is precise.

- "He is always well prepared for meetings and can justify his viewpoint." In order to be more constructive in the meetings, I always make preparation work before a meeting. I wrote down all questions where I would like to get answers, I prepare necessary data that can help analyze situation and make decision, I think about possible solution that we can use, and so on. Thus, I am always ready to answer on specific questions in meetings and ready to strongly argue my viewpoint.

- "He is always friendly, open, and positive. It is easy to communicate with him." I am positively minded. It helps me to move further through everyday life. Also, it helps in the communication process with other people because I am seeking for win–win situations where both parties become satisfied.
- "He is loyal to the company." As the company hired me, I am loyal to this company, and all my activities are directed for the interests of the company. Also, as the person, I am honest and never cheat. However, if needed for the company, I can bluff; that is completely different approach comparing with lying.
- "He is correct and hold in respect others." I have respect toward other people, regardless of their social status. Also, lower-level employees in our company produce certain result that is important in order to achieve main targets. Even if somebody makes mistake, I am not the judge who has to punish him. I can indicate him how to avoid mistakes in the future and improve performance.

Private

I asked for positive feedback about me from my family (wife and children) and friends. This feedback I received directly and by word of mouth. Thus, I will use a form *you*:

- "You have a good sense of humor." I can make different people laughing. Certainly I can be and I am serious in the important meetings, for example, with collaboration partners. However, if I see that a bit of cheerfulness will help to maintain a non-stressful atmosphere, then I naturally utilize my sense of humor even in these meetings.
- "You spend much time with children despite hard load at work." Certainly, the work itself is important, as it provides financial resources for me and my family. However, the family is the most important in my life, and thus, they get majority

of my out of office time. I enjoy talking and playing with my kids and they also enjoy it.

- "It is interesting to spend time with you because you are always oriented on some activities." I prefer any activities comparing with sitting, eating, drinking, and talking. I would say that I am always in motion. Either these are some sport activities or playing table games or playing outdoor games, like photo hunting, and so on

- "You take care of your physical shape." I need a lot of internal energy in order to use it externally. Physical activities are the way how I can supplement the level of my internal energy. I am cycling in the summertime, going to swimming pool in the wintertime, and playing table tennis throughout the year.

APPENDIX 7

Guiding Questionnaire for Personal Reflection

Dear reader,

The time for personal reflection has as an objective to help you in analyzing your current challenges and your attitudes towards them. The following questions are inserted only to orientate your task but you could skip some or all of them if you feel they are not of help. They are prepared based on the experience of many counselors, professors and experts in human resources and leadership.

The first message this questionnaire wants to convey is that any serious and substantial change at your organization starts with the willingness of all its members to improve personally in the exercise of their responsibilities, big or small ones. At the end of the day the performance of a whole organization is not more than the sum of the performance of all its members, it doesn't matter how important their tasks look like.

- ✓ Am I aware of my dignity, and of the power of my mind, heart and will? Am I aware of my personal freedom to take every single decision?
- ✓ I have been called to do great things, above all, to develop my personality and that of those around me. Do I know this?
- ✓ Do I realize that I am responsible for the fate of those around me?
- ✓ Do I have confidence in myself, and in my talents and abilities?
- ✓ Reflection and action are linked. Do I reflect before I act? Does reflection give rise to and inform my actions? By the same token, does action foster in me a reflexive spirit?

✓ Do I set high goals for myself and others? Do I strive, daily, to improve my character and behavior?

✓ Do I know what I am good at doing? Have I ever asked my friends, colleagues or adviser to help me discover what I am good at, and to improve?

✓ As important as it is to struggle against my defects, I should be more concerned to develop and augment my strengths. Am I?

✓ Do I devote enough time to considering my personal and professional mission? Have I discerned a mission in life?

✓ Do I focus on accomplishing my mission, or do I become distracted by peripheral matters?

✓ Do I try to inspire a sense of mission in my friends, work and colleagues?

✓ Am I able to make bold decisions or am I risk-averse? Does my fear of making mistakes cause me to be indecisive?

✓ Do I see obstacles as summits to be conquered, or do I give in to pessimism?

✓ Do I seek to address the problems of my workplace, society, country, humanity? Do I see them as opportunities to grow?

✓ The only thing I have to fear is not the evil that others do, but the good I fail to do. Do I realize this?

✓ Do I respect the dignity of others, especially the ones I lead? Do I lead by example rather than compulsion, do I teach rather than command, inspire rather than browbeat? Leadership is less about displays of power than about the empowerment of others. Am I aware of this and do I act accordingly?

✓ Do I solicit the input of others in solving problems? Do I make use of their contributions?

✓ Do I refrain from interfering in the work of my subordinates, unless I have good reason? Do I avoid treating them like children?

✓ Do I avoid the temptation to do subordinates' work for them?

✓ Do I readily delegate power, that is, transfer decision-making power to subordinates?

✓ Do I foster in my team a culture of freedom and personal responsibility so that everyone truly participates in decision-making and feels accountable?

✓ Do I do everything I can to strengthen the commitment of team members to the shared mission?

✓ Do I draw out the reticent, encourage the domineering to yield, and help pessimists to see the positive side? Do I urge them to question the conventional wisdom?

✓ Do I renounce my judgments (unless principles are at stake) when the group decides against my position? If, subsequently, decision taken against my advice proves mistaken, do avoid saying, "I told you so"? Do I participate enthusiastically in the implementation of all decisions—even those I initially opposed?

✓ Do I promote my workplace rather than myself? Do I avoid making myself indispensable? Do I share information? Do I create the conditions whereby others can successfully finish what I started?

✓ Do I choose my collaborators well, and pave the way for my succession? Do I find, develop and encourage new leaders?

✓ Do I take pleasure in being of service? Do I cultivate altruistic motives?

✓ The employee who is motivated by a desire to serve is better suited for a leadership position than one more concerned to seek material rewards, no matter how brilliant his professional background. Am I aware of this?

✓ Am I concerned that those who work for and with me are happy? Do I take a proper interest in their professional success and financial security? I am prepared to do what I can to help them achieve happiness in their personal lives? Am I loyal to them?

✓ Do I learn from those I lead?

References

n.d. Retrieved from Barret Values Center: www.valuescentre.com/mapping-values/values

Aktaş, Y.A. March 20, 2018. "Medium Corporation." Available at https://medium.com/@yinalardanakta/natural-disasters-02-earthquakes-b98ef0d96e0a

Bennis, W., and G. Joan. 1997. *Learning to Lead*. Cambridge, Massachusetts: Perseus Books.

Bryant. November 26, 2011. "The Importance of Painting a Clear Picture." Retrieved from https://nytimes.com/2011/11/27/business/electronic-arts-chief-on-painting-a-consistent-picture.html

Cambridge English Dictionary. n.d. "Self-Efficacy." Available at https://dictionary.cambridge.org/dictionary/english/self-efficacy

Caritas. n.d. "Video: One Human Family, Food for All." Available at https://food.caritas.org/video-one-human-family-food-for-all/

Carnegie Mellon University. n.d. "Randy Pausch's Last Lecture." Available at https://cmu.edu/randyslecture/

Centre, B.V. n.d. Available at www.valuescentre.com/mapping-values/values

Chopra. March 2014. "Is Critical Thinking Being Outsourced to Google?" Available at https://linkedin.com/pulse/20140301230842-17584873-is-critical-thinking-being-outsourced-to-google/

Covey, S. 1998. *The 7 Habits of Highly Effective People*.

Drucker, P.F. 1973. *Management*. Allied Publishers Private Limited.

Dyer, J., H. Gregersen, and C.M. Christensen. 2011. "The Innovator's DNA." Available at http://library.globalchalet.net/Authors/Startup%20Collection/%5BDyer%20et%20al.,%202011%5D%20The%20Innovator's%20DNA%20-%20Mastering%20the%20Five%20Skills%20of%20Disruptive%20Innovators.pdf

Eblin, S. October 9, 2017. "How to Determine If the Balls You're Juggling are Rubber or Glass." Available at LinkedIn: https://linkedin.com/pulse/how-determine-balls-youre-juggling-rubber-glass-scott-eblin

Every Day Scientist. n.d. "SAM'S CV of Failures." Retrieved from http://everydayscientist.com/CV/sjl_CV-failures.pdf

Frankl, V. 2017. *Man's Search for Meaning*. Beacon Press.

Fullan, M. 2013. *Educational Leadership*. The Jossey-Bass Reader.

Gandz, J. 2006. "Are you a Leader-Breeder?" Available at IVEY Business Journal: https://iveybusinessjournal.com/publication/are-you-a-leader-breeder/

García-Lombardía, P., and P. Cardona. 2005. *How to Develop Leadership Competencies.* Navarra: EUNSA.

Gardner, H. 2011. *Frames of Mind: The Theory of Multiple Intelligences.* Basic Books.

Goleman, D. 2006. *Emotional Intelligence.* Bantam Books.

Greenleaf, R.K. 1970. *The Servant as a Leader.* Greenleaf Center For Servant Leadership.

Havard, A. 2007. *Virtuous Leadership.* Scepter.

Hemingway, E.M. n.d. Available at Poetry Foundation: https://poetryfoundation.org/poets/ernest-m-hemingway

Hofstede-Insights. n.d. Available at https://hofstede-insights.com/product/compare-countries/

Keirsey Temperament Sorter. n.d. Available at keirsey.com/temperament-overview/

Kotter, J.P. 1990. *A Force for Change. How Leadership Differs from Management.* New York, NY: The Free Press.

Krell, D.F. 1990. *Of Memory, Reminiscence, and Writing: On the Verge.* Indiana University Press.

Larburu, A. 2005. *Foundations of Coaching.* IESE.

Layard, R. n.d. "The Secrets of Happiness." Available at https://open.edu/openlearn/ocw/pluginfile.php/624971/mod_resource/content/1/gsg_3_reading1.pdf

Lewis, C. May 3, 2017. Available at the Abolition of Man: https://bookdepository.com/Abolition-Man-C-S-Lewis/9781681090092

Luft, J. 1969. *Of Human Interaction.* Mayfield.

Metropolitan Museum of Art. n.d. Available at https://metmuseum.org/art/collection/search/226600

MindTools. n.d. "Personal SWOT Analysis Making the Most of Your Talents and Opportunities." Available at https://mindtools.com/pages/article/newTMC_05_1.htm

Nash, L., and H. Stevenson. 2005. *Just Enough: Tools for Creating Success in Your Work and Life.* John Wiley & Sons.

Nietzsche, F. 1974. *Twilight of the Idols: Or, How to Philosophise with the Hammer.* Gordon Press.

Nuria, C., and M. Maruja. 2013. *Masters of Our Destiny.* Eunsa.

Pascal, B., H. Rogers, V. Cousin, and C. Louandre. 1861. *The Thoughts, Letters and Opuscules of Blaise Pascal.* H.W. Derby.

Pree, M. 1987. *Leadership is an Art.* Michigan State University Press.

Rajadhyaksha, U. 2005. *Managerial Competence: Do Technical Capabilities Matter?*

Rivera, C.A. 2013. *Building a Model of Leadership Development For Times of Change*. Drukatava.

Seligman, M. 2017. *Authentic Happiness: Using the New Positive Psychology to Realize your Potential for Deep Fulfilment*. Nicholas Brealey.

Siegel, L. n.d. "Groucho Marx: The Comedy of Existence." Available at https://vitalsource.com/de/en-GB/products/groucho-marx-the-comedy-of-existence-lee-siegel-v9780300216639

Stanford Graduate School of Business. 2012. "Leadership In Focus." Available at https://leadershipinfocus.net/presentations/video-cases/

Thomson, J.J. 1985. "The Trolley Problem." Available at http://library.du.edu

Thurman, H. May 4, 1980. "Baccalaureate Address at Spelman College." Available at https://uindy.edu/eip/files/reflection4.pdf

Virtuous Leadership Institute. 2017. "History: What is Virtuous Leadership?" Available at https://virtuousleadership.org/history

Von Goethe, J.W. 1853. *Goethe's Opinions on the World, Mankind, Literature, Science, and Art*. John W. Parker and Son.

Warner Bros. n.d. Available at https://warnerbros.com/citizen-kane

World Economic Forum. n.d. "New Vision for Education." Retrieved from https://widgets.weforum.org/nve-2015/chapter1.html

About the Authors

Claudio A. Rivera, PhD

Educator, Writer, Social Innovator

RTU Riga Business School Associate Professor in Leadership and Director of the University of New York at Buffalo/RBS Bachelor's Programs in Business and IT. He is also the Lead of Education for the Foreign Investors Council in Latvia. As such, he is one of the leaders in the design of one of the most significant reforms in higher education since the regaining of the independence.

Claudio has a long track of experience in public speaking, consulting, and research. He has also successfully founded several social ventures connected with education and innovation. As a professor, Claudio has developed several leadership programs and has been teaching in many countries in Europe, Latin America, and Africa. He has published extensively, including five books as author and coauthor.

His main areas of interests are youth development, social entrepreneurship, interdisciplinary education, servant leadership, and social innovation.

Elza Priede, MBA

Educator, Connector, Youth Mentor

RTU Riga Business School Community Manager. Elza has spent most of her career working with the current and the next generation of Baltic civic and business leaders—Riga Business School's Executive MBA, MBA, and BSc students. During her time at Riga Business School, Elza has played an integral role in the development and execution of the BSc programs. One of Elza's career passions is helping to guide entrepreneurs-to-be through the thought process involved in integrating social responsibility and entrepreneurship, for example, building their study and career roadmaps, developing an entrepreneurial attitude, enhancing their leadership capacities and confidence, self-awareness, social awareness, and responsibility. Elza holds an MBA in Marketing and IT from Riga Business School; she is a Baltic-American Freedom Foundation Professional Internship Program Alumna and Riga Business School MBA Programs Ambassador. As a youth mentor, Elza has been a part of the development of multiple mentorship programs for business school students, disadvantaged youth in Latvia, and worked within the Council on International Educational Exchange, in the United States.

Her professional interests include youth development, mentorship, transformational leadership, social progress, meaningful educational exchange, social and educational innovation.

Index

OTHER TITLES IN THE BUSINESS CAREER DEVELOPMENT COLLECTION

Vilma Barr, Consultant, Editor

- *The Champion Edge* by Alan R. Zimmerman
- *Your GPS to Employment Success* by Beverly A. Williams
- *Getting It Right When It Matters Most* by Tony Gambill and Scott Carbonara
- *How to Make Good Business Decisions* by J.C. Baker
- *100 Skills of the Successful Sales Professional* by Alex Dripchak
- *Personal and Career Development* by Claudio A. Rivera and Elza Priede
- *Rules Don't Work for Me* by Gail Summers
- *Finding Your Career Niche* by Anne S. Klein
- *Shaping Your Future* by Rita Rocker-Craft
- *Emotional Intelligence at Work* by Richard M. Contino and Penelope J. Holt
- *The Trust Factor* by Russell von Frank
- *Creating A Business and Personal Legacy* by Mark J. Munoz
- *Innovative Selling* by Eden White
- *Present! Connect!* by Tom Guggino
- *Introduction to Business* by Patrice Flynn
- *Be Different!* by Stan Silverman

Concise and Applied Business Books

The Collection listed above is one of 30 business subject collections that Business Expert Press has grown to make BEP a premiere publisher of print and digital books. Our concise and applied books are for...

- Professionals and Practitioners
- Faculty who adopt our books for courses
- Librarians who know that BEP's Digital Libraries are a unique way to offer students ebooks to download, not restricted with any digital rights management
- Executive Training Course Leaders
- Business Seminar Organizers

Business Expert Press books are for anyone who needs to dig deeper on business ideas, goals, and solutions to everyday problems. Whether one print book, one ebook, or buying a digital library of 110 ebooks, we remain the affordable and smart way to be business smart. For more information, please visit www.businessexpertpress.com, or contact sales@businessexpertpress.com.

www.ingramcontent.com/pod-product-compliance
Lightning Source LLC
Chambersburg PA
CBHW061153220326
41599CB00025B/4466